W9-CCN-549

Preparing
Children

for Success
in School and Life

WITHDRAWN

WITHDRAWN

MARCIA L. TATE

Preparing Children

for Success

in School and Life

20 WAYS TO INCREASE YOUR CHILD'S BRAIN POWER

Foreword by Eric Jensen

CORWIN
A SAGE Company

CORWIN
A SAGE Company

FOR INFORMATION:

Corwin
A SAGE Company
2455 Teller Road
Thousand Oaks, California
91320
(800) 233-9936
Fax: (800) 417-2466
www.corwin.com

SAGE Ltd.
1 Oliver's Yard
55 City Road
London EC1Y 1SP
United Kingdom

SAGE India Pvt. Ltd.
B 1/I 1 Mohan Cooperative
Industrial Area
Mathura Road, New Delhi
110 044
India

SAGE Asia-Pacific Pte. Ltd.
33 Pekin Street #02-01
Far East Square
Singapore 048763

Acquisitions Editor: Carol Collins
Associate Editor: Megan Bedell
Editorial Assistant: Sarah Bartlett
Production Editor: Veronica Stapleton
Copy Editor: Kim Husband
Typesetter: C&M Digitals (P) Ltd.
Proofreader: Gretchen Treadwell
Indexer: Diggs Publication Services
Cover Designer: Rose Storey
Graphic Designer: Adele Hutchinson

Copyright © 2011 by Corwin

All rights reserved. When forms and sample documents are included, their use is authorized only by educators, local school sites, and/or noncommercial or nonprofit entities that have purchased the book. Except for that usage, no part of this book may be reproduced or utilized in any form or by any means, electronic or mechanical, including photocopying, recording, or by any information storage and retrieval system, without permission in writing from the publisher.

All trade names and trademarks recited, referenced, or reflected herein are the property of their respective owners who retain all rights thereto.

Printed in the United States of America

Library of Congress Cataloging-in-Publication Data

Tate, Marcia L.
Preparing children for success in school and life : 20 ways to enhance your child's brain power/ Marcia L. Tate; foreword by Eric Jensen.

p. cm.
Includes bibliographical references and index.

ISBN 978-1-4129-8844-5 (pbk.)

1. Child development. 2. Children—Intelligence levels. 3. Cognition in children. 4. Parenting. 5. Education—Parent participation. I. Title.

HQ767.9.T38 2011
649'.1—dc23   2011019157

This book is printed on acid-free paper

11 12 13 14 15 10 9 8 7 6 5 4 3 2 1

Contents

64(.1
TAT

Foreword

Marcia Tate has done it again! Parents, look no further. In these pages, she addresses children's very first teachers, and the result is a quality feast of relevant information for any parent. Three big things in the book blew me away.

First, the information is absolutely relevant and laser focused. It is exactly what you need to know as a parent and nothing more. There is not a single wasted page and everything that is included is valuable.

Second, the information is quality. A peerless educator as always, Marcia has done her homework and incorporated the most up-to-date information available. I saw fresh ideas that every parent must know on page after page.

Third, three timeless but essential themes of wise and successful childrearing—heart, health, and brain—are touchstones throughout the book. You'll learn how to build cognition and creativity in your child's brain as well as how to foster optimal emotional and physical development.

It's refreshing to encounter such a positive and grounded assumption that you can learn how to develop a better relationship with your child. You'll learn how to surround your child with a calming environment and how to give your child a brain-healthy start. The book's many detailed and practical chapters invite you to talk to and teach your child critical life rules, rituals, and responsibility. These topics are both urgent and embedded in everyday family life. Threaded throughout is the reminder that, as a parent, you have the power to accentuate the positive and deemphasize the negative. You can learn how to expect the best and visualize success.

This practical book will help you identify chronic behavior and mood disorders and identify and strengthen your child's auditory, visual, or tactile mode of learning. Memories with music close out the book, and it's a key part to a happy childhood in the making, mindfully overseen.

Finally, this book is a "take action" book. You'll get excited about the information and you'll want to put it into practice. Indeed, you're nudged to take action to ensure it happens. This is a book that will move you to do the right thing and do it more often.

If I sound a bit gushy about the book, it's because it's a triumph. Marcia has taken a tough topic and caught the magic for your reading pleasure. I know you'll enjoy this feast as much as I have. Bon appétit!

—Eric Jensen, author and consultant

Acknowledgments

Being an effective parent is probably more difficult today than ever before. However, there are people who are doing it well on a daily basis. Families come in all shapes and sizes. There are two-parent, single-parent, and foster families; there are grandmothers and grandfathers, aunts, uncles, sisters, and brothers who all fulfill the critical role of *parent*. You see, true parents are not the people who simply give birth. Parents are the people who strive to meet the everyday physical, mental, social, and emotional needs of the beautiful children who are blessed to be within their care.

This book is dedicated to those parents who desire to become better at what they do daily. It is my belief that no matter how great a parent one strives to be, each day, that parent should set specific goals to become better. This book will enable you to do just that! With the world changing as it is, if we are not working to improve, then we begin to move backward. I strive every day to become a better daughter, wife, mother, grandmother, sister, and friend to the important people in my life.

This book is also devoted to my parents, Alvin, a Methodist minister under whose administration two churches were built in the Atlanta, Georgia, area and Eurica, my mother and Alvin's devoted wife for more than 35 years before he passed away. My parents equipped me and my two sisters, Ann and Eleanor, with values, morals, and the belief that we were capable of accomplishing whatever we put our minds to and worked hard to achieve. We all have been very successful both professionally and personally, in great part thanks to them!

This book is also dedicated to our three children, Jennifer, Jessica, and Christopher, of whom I am most proud. As parents, there were times when Tyrone and I were not necessarily at our best but, despite our efforts, you persevered and you should be pleased with the wonderful adult human beings you have become. When I look at you, I realize that your dad and I must have done something right. You are also making wonderful parents for your own children, Christian and Aidan, our grandchildren.

I owe a tremendous debt of gratitude to Corwin Press, particularly Carol Collins, my editor, for being willing to take a chance and allowing me to write the first book published by Corwin strictly for parents. I am honored to be its author and feel that it has the capability to make a positive difference in the lives of parents and their children everywhere.

PUBLISHER'S ACKNOWLEDGMENTS

Corwin gratefully acknowledges the contributions of the following reviewers:

Patricia Baker, Kindergarten–Fifth Grade Teacher
Mary Walter Elementary School
Culpeper, VA

Nic Cooper, Faculty
Teacher Preparation Program
Baker College
Jackson, MI

Eleonora di Liscia, Attorney
Skokie, IL

Michelle Webb, Graphic Designer
Thousand Oaks, CA

About the Author

Marcia L. Tate, EdD, is the former executive director of professional development for the DeKalb County School System, Decatur, Georgia. During her 30-year career with the district, she has been a classroom teacher, reading specialist, language arts coordinator, and staff development executive director. She received the Distinguished Staff Development Award for the State of Georgia, and her department was chosen to receive the Exemplary Program Award for the state. More important, Marcia has been married to Tyrone Tate for more than 30 years and is the proud mother of three wonderful adult children: Jennifer, Jessica, and Christopher; and the doting grandmother of two granddaughters, Christian and Aidan.

Marcia is currently an educational consultant and has taught more than 350,000 parents, teachers, administrators, and business and community leaders throughout the world, including Australia, Egypt, Hungary, Singapore, Thailand, and New Zealand. She is the author of the following five bestsellers: *Worksheets Don't Grow Dendrites: 20 Instructional Strategies That Engage the Brain; "Sit & Get" Won't Grow Dendrites: 20 Professional Learning Strategies That Engage the Adult Brain; Reading and Language Arts Worksheets Don't Grow Dendrites: 20 Literacy Strategies That Engage the Brain; Shouting Won't Grow Dendrites: 20 Techniques for Managing a Brain-Compatible Classroom;* and *Mathematics Worksheets Don't Grow Dendrites: 20 Numeracy Strategies That Engage the Brain.* Her most recent book is *Science Worksheets Don't Grow Dendrites: 20 Instructional Strategies That Engage the Brain,* cowritten with Warren Phillips, one of the best science teachers in the country. Participants refer to her workshops as some of the best they have ever experienced, since Marcia uses the 20 brain-compatible strategies outlined in her books to actively engage her audiences.

Marcia received her bachelor's degree in psychology and elementary education from Spelman College in Atlanta, Georgia. She earned her master's degree in remedial reading from the University of Michigan, her specialist degree in educational leadership from Georgia State University, and her doctorate in educational leadership from Clark Atlanta University. Spelman College awarded her the Apple Award for excellence in the field of education.

Marcia and her husband own the consulting firm Developing Minds Inc. and can be contacted by calling (770) 918-5039 or by e-mail: marciata@bellsouth.net. Visit her website at www.developing mindsinc.com.

Introduction

What if the following advertisement appeared in your local paper:

WANTED: PARENT

Must have the skills of a doctor, lawyer, nurse, teacher, counselor, and referee

Must maintain a sense of humor even in the most stressful times

Must be able to operate a taxi service to and from all important events

No pay, lots of overtime

In fact, on call 24 hours a day

No sick days allowed

Lifetime commitment

(Tate, 2007, p. 121)

If this ad recruiting people to become parents appeared in the paper, would anyone ever apply? Yet parents are asked to fulfill these responsibilities and many more each and every day. More than 30 years of being a wife and mother to three children has taught me one thing: being a good parent is one of the hardest jobs on the face of the earth. With negative role models abounding, violence and negativity in the media increasing, and our face-to-face communication diminishing, the job of a parent appears to be getting more difficult each year. Yet it is one of the most important and rewarding jobs one can undertake and it is absolutely crucial that it be done well!

PARENTS AS DENDRITE GROWERS

A baby is born with approximately one hundred billion neurons, or memory cells. In fact, in utero, each fetus has more than one hundred billion neurons, but some are pruned away, or discarded, prior to birth. At the end of every neuron are connections called dendrites. Every time the human brain learns something new, it grows a new dendrite. Messages are passed from one neuron to another as those messages travel from the cell body, down the axon, across the synapse, or space between the two neurons, and into the dendrite of the next neuron. (See the diagram below.)

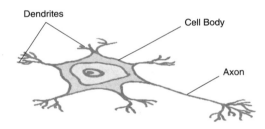

Many parents have the attitude that it is the school's responsibility to be the primary educator of their children while they play a minor, although important, supporting role (Glasgow & Whitney, 2009). Actually, we know that the most rapid period of growth for cells in the human brain is 0 to 4 years of age. That would make a parent a child's first and best teacher. Parents as well as teachers are *dendrite growers*, since every time they enable their children to learn something new, they help them to grow new dendrites and increase their brain power.

During my 37 years in education, I have seen numerous examples of children whose parents implemented the practices in this book and who, regardless of race, religion, or socioeconomic status, produced children who were equipped for success not only in school but in life. Yet many other parents simply don't know what to do nor are they familiar with the practices essential for raising successful offspring. Am I a perfect parent? Not by any stretch of the imagination. But I have managed to raise three well-adjusted and respectful children who, I am proud to say, have become wonderful adults and two of the three are great parents themselves. The other one does not yet have children.

OVERVIEW OF THE BOOK

This book is divided into two major parts. The first part deals with what parents should be doing from birth on to prepare their children to lead successful lives. It is a compilation of what we are learning about brain research and selected effective practices from several different programs designed to make one an effective person as well as an effective parent. The second major part shares brain-compatible strategies for increasing the academic achievement of your children and designates ways that you can prepare your children to be successful in school and, ultimately, in whatever career path they undertake.

The format of this book is similar to that of the five bestsellers in the *Worksheets* series I have written. The first part of each chapter will define the recommended practice in a simple and brain-friendly way and will share current research from the fields of psychology and education regarding the rationale for using the practice. The second part in each chapter will provide numerous examples of ways you and your children can use the practice. The last page in each chapter asks that you reflect on the practice and how you may be able to personally apply it in your home through an *action plan*. Remember that it takes approximately 21 days or 28 times to make a behavior a habit. So the action steps that you identify should be practiced continuously. It is my hope that by the time you complete this book, you will not only know more of what to do and how to do it but will also develop an action plan of specific steps for improving your individual parenting skills.

The final part of the book contains a *contract* that I am asking you to sign as a commitment to becoming better at being a parent. Remember, no matter how good a parent each of us becomes, each day, we should strive to become better ones! Our children certainly deserve no less!

PART ONE

Preparing Children for Success in Life

To understand the purpose of this book, we will use the strategies of storytelling, visualization, and metaphor. Visualize, if you will, two cans of Coca-Cola. One can is unopened and filled to the brim with liquid. The other can is totally empty. Imagine yourself taking your bare hands and attempting to crush the full can of Coke. Try as you might, it will be very difficult, at best, to crush the can. There may be a few dents or dings on the outside of the can, but the can itself will remain virtually intact. Now try to crush the empty can of Coke. It should be very easy to collapse the sides against one another since there is nothing inside the can to prevent you from doing so.

This demonstration is a metaphor for the way some parents choose to raise their children. Like the full can of Coca-Cola, some parents *fill their children* with the principles essential for a successful life. Therefore, when these children are bombarded by outside influences that would *crush their healthy* existence, such as negative peer pressure, inappropriate role models from the media, or enticements to engage in detrimental behavior, it may have little to no effect on their inner being. Other parents who do not take the time or bother to *fill their children* develop children who are easily crushed by outside influences or who look to other things to *fill their cans.*

This book will attempt to recommend essential strategies for *filling the cans* of your children. It is a compilation of the following life-changing programs I have been trained to teach to people around the world:

o Stephen Covey's *7 Habits of Highly Effective People* and *7 Habits of Highly Effective Families*

o Don Lowry's *True Colors*, a personality and temperament inventory that identifies the strengths and challenges of all people

o *The Power of Positive Thinking*, a course I developed based on the extraordinary things that happen when people think positively, as well as the original book of the same name by Dr. Norman Vincent Peale

o My book on classroom management, *Shouting Won't Grow Dendrites; 20 Techniques for Managing a Brain-compatible Classroom*

o My book on brain-compatible teaching, *Worksheets Don't Grow Dendrites: 20 Instructional Strategies that Engage the Brain*

o My personal experiences as a parent, teacher, administrator, and professional development leader for almost 40 years

These programs are replete with strategies for filling children of any age with the values and morals essential for healthy mental, physical, social, and spiritual growth and development. Enjoy your journey through the pages of this book and set goals to become a better parent and person for having read it!

Develop a Relationship With Your Child

Parents must work harder than ever at building satisfying and affirming relationships with their kids.

—Dobson, 2001

WHAT DOES THAT MEAN?

Since relationships form the basis of every interaction between human beings, it is only fitting that the initial chapter deal with the parent–child relationship. Relationships are everything! In fact, according to Runkel (2007) in his book, *Screamfree Parenting: The Revolutionary Approach to Raising Your Kids by Keeping Your Cool*, in relationship battles, there are no victors, only casualties. I have personally observed blended families where a stepparent moves into the home and does not bother to develop a relationship with the stepchildren. Then, when the stepparent tries to tell the stepchildren what to do or what time to be home, the reply becomes, *You can't tell me what to do! You are not my mother!* or *You are not my father!* On the other hand, when the stepparent takes the time and effort to bond with the stepchildren and develop a relationship with them, when the stepparent asks the children to do something or not to do something, they are more likely to comply. When our children know that they can trust us, they are more likely to do what we ask of them, especially if they know it is really important (Kohn, 2005). That trust builds with a sustained relationship.

There is a concept known as the *emotional bank account,* which I learned about as I was being trained to teach *The 7 Habits of Highly Effective People.* This concept literally changed our family life! The concept uses the brain strategy of metaphor and compares our relationships with people in life to a bank account, but not a monetary bank account; it is a relationship or emotional bank account. Just like with our financial account, we make emotional deposits and withdrawals as we interact with our family members, friends, coworkers, and others. If we experience more withdrawals, or negative interactions, with one another than deposits (positive interactions), then our mutual bank account is soon overdrawn. If we continue that practice, the relationship becomes bankrupt. That is what divorce is—a bankrupt relationship that experienced far more or larger withdrawals than deposits.

> When people have strong *emotional bank accounts* with other people through the deposits of courtesy, kindness, honesty, and keeping commitments, a reserve of trust is built up that compensates for any shortcomings. When the trust account is high, communication is easy and effective (Covey, 2004).

Parents who have strong relationships with their children make far more deposits than withdrawals on a daily basis. Yet what do you think is the average number of minutes per day that fathers spend in meaningful conversation with their children? If you guessed 7 minutes, then you would be correct. For mothers, it is not much better—approximately 11 minutes. If you spend more time than that with your children, reach across your body with your dominant hand and pat yourself on the back.

> Strong marriages have at least a five-to-one daily ratio of positive to negative interactions (Parker-Pope, 2010).

Who determines what constitutes a deposit or a withdrawal? If you said the recipient, then you would be correct. Therefore, you have to really know your children to know what they would consider positive or negative interactions with you. However, there are a few things most people would regard as deposits. These include courtesy toward one another, quality time engaged in meaningful activities, attendance at extracurricular or school events, establishing a trusting relationship, recognition for a job well done, and being a good listener. Being a great parent requires more listening than talking and not being so busy trying to get our children to see our point of view that we neglect hearing theirs (Kohn, 2005).

Here is a true story. My husband and I were eating dinner at a local restaurant in Atlanta, Georgia, when I noticed a family of four sitting at a nearby table. The family consisted of a father, mother, and two teenage sons. We sat and ate for more than an hour and I observed that the family members said no more than several words to one another during the entire time. You see, the father was reading the newspaper, the mother was eating and staring into space, one son had ear buds in his ears and was listening to his iPod, and the other was alternately eating and text messaging. I thought to myself, *This is a sign of our times.* This family just missed a prime opportunity to talk with and listen to their teenagers—to find out what is going on in their lives, who their friends are, how school is going, or what their future dreams are. Yet none of those conversations took place. Everyone was caught up in his or her own personal activities.

Is it any wonder that teenagers spend time talking with strangers on the Internet? One of the five basic needs of the human brain is the need to belong, to have someone to talk with and someone who will also listen. The problem is that when that someone is a stranger, the conversation may lead to a dangerous liaison. Find quality time to spend with your children. It will pay huge dividends toward a meaningful relationship.

> Teenagers have a very strong need to interact with positive adult role models even if they make it appear that they do not need adults (Adamson, Hartman, & Lyxsell, 1999).

Many parents try to substitute things (clothes, toys, electronic gadgets, and so forth) for time, thinking that material possessions will make their children happy. Things may make people happy temporarily, but the joy is short-lived! Have you ever noticed that some of the unhappiest people in the world have the most money and the greatest number of personal possessions? If you will admit it, the fondest memories you have from your childhood are not from things that you received but from time you spent with the important people in your life.

Put first things first! Make quality time to spend with your family. I doubt that any person comes to the end of his or her life and makes the following statement to loved ones gathered nearby: *I wish I had spent more time at the office!* Most of the regrets come from missed opportunities with the family and friends you love! Remember that *your children do not care how much you know until they know how much you care!*

HOW CAN I MAKE IT HAPPEN?

o   Make more deposits than withdrawals in the bank accounts of your family members. For every negative interaction, there should be 5 to 10 positive interactions. In other words, for every time you must tell your children something for their own good, there should be 5 to 10 times when you are telling them or showing them how special they are to you. I will never forget the time that my husband made a major deposit in our daughter Jessica's bank account. Jessica's date for the senior prom became ill at the last minute and could not take her. Since we knew that it was too late for her to get another date, on prom night, Jessica's dad invited her to become his dinner date at one of Atlanta's best restaurants. He even cleaned up the car and purchased a wrist corsage just for her. After dinner, her dad dropped Jessica at the prom and she rode home later with friends. Neither Jessica nor her dad will ever forget the special evening that they spent together! What a deposit in both of their bank accounts! That major deposit alone increased the amount of contact that Jess and her father had after she left home for college.

o   Whenever possible, have dinner together as a family. Be sure that children and parents assist in the preparation of the dinner, setting the table, and clearing the dishes. Each family member should have a designated job to do, which makes the whole experience easier for everyone. If this week, it is one child's turn to set the table, next week that same child may be the one who puts the dishes in the dishwasher. It is not the dinner that makes the difference, it is the quality time spent in conversation around the table that matters most! In fact, when National Merit Finalists were compared with one another, one of the major characteristics they had in common was their daily conversations with family members around the dinner table.

○ When it is not possible to have dinner together as a family, due to work, church, or school commitments or to extracurricular activities, find other times to work on your relationship with your children. One ideal time to have these conversations is in the car. Turn off the radio and DVD player, have your children put down the cell phone, and talk with them in the car. Ask them about their school day, their friends, their aspirations and short- and long-term goals, and allow them to talk to you about what they wish. Remember to do at least as much listening as you do talking—maybe even more!

○ Designate a specific night of the week as *family night*. Make this night a priority and let nothing keep any member of the family from being available during this time. Plan an activity that the family can engage in together such as dinner out at a restaurant, popcorn and a movie, or a night of bowling. The family may want to spend this night at home watching a video that family members take turns selecting or playing board games such as Monopoly, Scattergories, Scrabble, or Taboo. When my children were all living at home, Friday night was *game night*. On Friday night, the children did not have to complete homework and my husband and I tried not to schedule meetings so that we could all be home together. We would play games and have fun! When I began to work on my doctorate, game night did not happen as often and I did not realize how much my children missed it until the day my 8-year-old son asked, *Mom, why are we not playing games anymore?* Now that they are grown, we still value those times and we still play games when they come over to visit. My daughters, son-in-law, and I are very evenly matched in a competitive game of Scrabble. My husband and I play backgammon, and my husband and his brother Greg play chess.

○ Board and card games are even good for parents. They are one of the 10 things that keep people living beyond the age of 80 (Mahoney, 2005). Remember, you don't stop playing games because you grow old. You grow old because you stop playing games. Games encourage social interaction and higher-level thinking and are loads of fun!

○ Make dates with your children periodically. If you have more than one child, make a date with each one separately. Since no two children, even twins, are exactly alike, allow your children to determine what they would like to do on their date with mom or dad. Then enjoy the company of each child and make him or her feel special since you are giving your time to only them.

○ Make dates with your spouse. My husband and I have been married for more than 30 years, and we still make dates. I travel a great deal, and he and I make a point of designating time most weekends to spend with one another. The date can consist of a meal out at a fancy restaurant or it can be as simple as a night watching a sporting event together on television while munching on goodies. By the way, I did not even like football until I married my husband many years ago. Now, it is one of my favorite sports. We even have season tickets to the Falcons games, which we attend with our daughter Jennifer, son-in-law Lex, and grand-daughter Aidan.

○ Let your children know that you are there for them and if they have a problem, they can come to you. Then when they come to you, be truly there for them. Put all work, chores, and cell phones aside and really listen! Try to seek first to understand what the problem is by actively listening as they talk. Ask questions for clarification, but don't even attempt to help in solving the problem until you are clear about what the problem entails and until you have encouraged your child to share his or her own thoughts about how the problem should be handled. Then work together to find a solution.

If you are a single parent, you may need to provide a positive male or female role model for your children. The Big Brothers and Big Sisters organizations can assist you in supplying a man who can develop a relationship that may make a positive difference in the life of your son or a woman who can make a positive difference in the life of your daughter. While there are boys who experience life positively without a male figure, increasing bodies of research across disciplines are showing that boys need positive male role models along the way (Nagel, 2006).

> The happiest and healthiest adolescents are raised by parents who talk through problems with them when they occur and use their control, not to discipline but to guide their teenagers (Feinstein, 2009).

○ Companies have mission statements, and so do some people. More than 10 years ago, I wrote my personal mission statement. Why not gather your children together when they are old enough to understand the task and work as a family to write a family mission statement? This statement is based on universal principles and should reflect what you are all about as a family and what your major contribution to society should be. In his book, *The 7 Habits of Highly Effective Families* (Covey, 1997), Stephen Covey discusses this task in depth and shows several examples of how to go about writing this statement. When I teach the course, *The 7 Habits of Highly Effective People*, one task for the class is to write their personal mission statements. One teacher in a class many years ago described his mission in one sentence, quoting a popular bumper sticker: *I want to be the kind of person that my dog already thinks I am.* Enough said!

○ Schedule family meetings periodically, perhaps once per month, when the entire family can get together and discuss accomplishments and challenges of the family during the last month. Allow children who are old enough to express their opinions and add to the discussion. If the family has written a mission statement, this is a good time to see what progress has been made in accomplishing the family's mission or purpose.

ACTION PLAN

> What will I commit to do to ensure that I develop a meaningful relationship with my child(ren)?

What am I already doing that I should continue to do?

1. _____
_____
_____.

2. _____
_____
_____.

3. _____
_____
_____.

4. _____
_____
_____.

What new habits will I commit to developing?

1. _____
_____
_____.

2. _____
_____
_____.

3. _____
_____
_____.

4. _____
_____
_____.

Hug, Rock, and Love Your Child

Since the brain is social and the body thrives with touch, young children need many hugs.

—Sprenger, 2008

WHAT DOES THAT MEAN?

I once heard a brain consultant by the name of Fritz Mengert say that if he had to choose between putting his grandchild in a day care center where teachers rock, hold, and hug children and one where the academics are first and foremost, the decision would not be a hard one. He would enroll his grandchild in the first one every time. After all, there are so many smart but crazy people in the world. The brain stands its best chance of growing normally if it is nurtured. Children tend to thrive in environments where there are various types of positive interactions. In fact, the greater the baby's stimulation through its senses of touch, smell, taste, hearing, and sight, the quicker its brain development (Fox, 2001).

The inverse is also true. I used to wonder why some people could do such mean and devastating things to other human beings and appear to feel no remorse or empathy. I now know that one of the reasons may be that they were not shown much empathy themselves. Some children who have never been rocked, held, touched in positive ways, and told that they matter can grow up without the empathy or sympathy that healthy brains develop. Since touch is a basic requirement for optimum health, both animal and human babies deprived of touch do not develop in normal ways (Weil, 2005). In fact, only one-fourth of children's brains are developed at birth. From birth on, every time a baby is fed, held, played with, talked to, sung to, or read to, the additional 75% develops. If you look at the personal history of many of the people who became serial killers, like Ted Bundy or Richard Ramirez, you will find that one of the correlates is often that they were verbally and/or physically abused in the early years of their upbringing when their ability to empathize was being developed.

> Empathy, or concern for others, may be hardwired in a baby's brain since it is one of the earliest emotions they display (Wingert & Brant, 2005).

Let's consider this analogy: What happens to pit bulls and other types of dogs who are groomed for dog fighting rings? They are both verbally and physically abused by people they trust. It makes the dogs so angry that they will often fight to the death. What makes us think the situation is any different for a human being? So many children are coming to school angry and oppositional, and some of these feelings may result from the lack of nurturing in the home.

Here is a personal true story. Our two daughters are our biological children. Our son, Christopher, is adopted. For almost the first year of his life, Chris was in a foster home with an elderly foster mother who fed and changed him and did little else. He was seldom talked to, read to, held, hugged, or rocked. When we adopted him, we discovered some deficits in his readiness for learning, for which we have attempted to compensate. His language skills were a bit delayed, his adenoids were blocking 20% of his hearing, and, as he grew up, he began to show symptoms of attention deficit disorder. While it is unclear whether these symptoms would have been present even if his initial environment had been a nurturing one, the great news is that we were able to make up a great deal of those deficits by surrounding him with lots of love, a multitude of hugs, plenty of talk, and constant attention. Even fear, rage, and separation systems formed at birth in some children can be controlled by responsive parents and attachment to a primary caregiver (Sunderland, 2006).

You have probably heard or read about the studies of babies born in orphanages that are fed and have their diapers changed but who are not touched, rocked, or held. The studies show that these babies do not seem to thrive as do those who receive personal attention.

If you don't commit to any other action plan in this book, please commit to continue to rock, hold, hug, and love your children. Human touch encourages healthy brain development. Networks of neurons, or brain cells, grow out of our experiences with senses and start forming patterns for learning (Hannaford, 2005). However, it doesn't matter how much children are loved by others such as grandparents or nannies; children need to know that they are loved by their parents first and foremost (Fox, 2001).

> Since touch activates numerous areas in the brain, premature babies who were not touched and held did not develop as rapidly as those who were (Rodriguez, 2007).

HOW CAN I MAKE IT HAPPEN?

○ Take time to hug, rock, hold, and love your newborn. Continue this practice throughout your baby's early life. Not only will it provide a sense of security for your child, but it can also lead to healthy brain development. In addition, babies who are not able to meet specific *emotional milestones* due to lack of touch could have difficulty learning to speak, read, and be successful later in school (Wingert & Brant, 2005, p. 35).

○ As children grow older, they do not lose their desire for positive interactions. However, those interactions may need to take another form. Give your older children high fives, pats on the back, and other forms of endearment. It will make a difference in your relationship with them.

○ Create a signal that only you and your children know that symbolizes your love and affection for one another. Use it at certain times throughout the day, such as when you are dropping your children off at school or taking them to a sporting event. For example, there used to be a television variety show called *The Carol Burnett Show*. Every time the show ended, Carol Burnett, its star, would pull her ear as she said *Goodnight.* This was her way of telling her grand-mother, who was always watching the show, that she loved her.

○ According to mental health professionals, people need approximately 12 positive interactions each day to thrive, 8 inter-actions to maintain their current state, and 4 interactions simply to survive. Positive interactions include smiles, hugs, handshakes, high fives, *I love yous*, and other affirming comments. Think of all the children who do not get a single positive interaction before they go to school. No one says *Good morning!* or *Have a great day!* Then they go to school, where they may get no positive interac-tions, and then return to the home where the interactions are still not forthcoming. No wonder the incidence of depression among children is increasing!

○ When you are angry with your children, this is the worst pos-sible time to discipline them. Increased anger is a threat to the brain. When the brain is threatened, it goes into survival mode and the blood moves downward from the parts of the brain where higher-level thinking takes place. People are unable to make rational decisions at this time and they will do or say things that they would never do or say if the brain were not in this state. Refer to Chapter 10 for additional information on responding negatively to inappropriate behavior.

○ The next time you get angry with your children, remember Habit 1 of *The 7 Habits Of Highly Effective People: be proactive, not reactive* (Covey, 2004). When a child misbehaves, proactive par-ents push the pause button and put some space between the mis-behavior and their response. In this space, they decide how they will deal with the misbehavior based on their principles. Reactive parents respond immediately and, for the reasons that we just discussed, that response is not usually the best one.

○ Refrain from using any forms of negative touch, such as pull-ing your children by their clothes or arms, shoving them, grabbing them, or spanking them. These negative interactions, if used exces-sively, can destroy parent–child relationships and create angry chil-dren who may even seek revenge for the actions of their parents.

○ When you are tempted to lose control of a situation with your children, remember this: *He who angers you controls you.* I have even seen children who purposefully did or said things in an effort to anger their parents. Remain calm! Don't let them push your buttons. Push the pause button instead! A teacher told me once, *They can't get your goat if they don't know where it is tied!*

ACTION PLAN

> What will I commit to do to ensure that my child(ren)
> are hugged, rocked, and loved?

What am I already doing that I should continue to do?

1. _____
   _____
   _____.

2. _____
   _____
   _____.

3. _____
   _____
   _____.

4. _____
   _____
   _____.

What new habits will I commit to developing?

1. _____
   _____
   _____.

2. _____
   _____
   _____.

3. _____
   _____
   _____.

4. _____
   _____
   _____.

Surround Your Child With a Calming Environment

*Music that gradually slows down has a compa-
rable relaxing effect on the brain.*

—Erlauer, 2003

WHAT DOES THAT MEAN?

Almost 10 years ago, my husband and I had dinner with good friends who had just purchased a new home. The walls of their dining room were painted a cranberry red and we dined in a beautifully exquisite setting. We loved the color so much that we decided to paint our den the same color. Bad idea! Our den had very high walls and ceilings, which meant that this energetic color proved overwhelming in a room that had once been the family's oasis of calm. Soon very little time was spent sitting in the den. Even the children avoided it! Needless to say, we soon repainted.

This incident occurred prior to my education about the impact of color, music, lighting, aromas, and seating on the brain. Less than

5 years later, we were able to build a house, and I worked with the builder to put my knowledge of these elements to practical use. Our current home is so brain-compatible that people who visit often comment about the fact that it is such a calming place to be. Let's examine the effects of these elements on your brain and how you might be able to use this information in creating a brain-compatible environment in your own home, not only for your children but for yourself as well. I must warn you, however, that one of the disadvantages of having a brain-compatible home is that when people visit, they like it so much that they will lengthen their stay!

Color

It is easy to remember the calming and high-energy colors if we simply look to the real world. If human beings were designed to commune with nature, wouldn't it make sense that the colors of nature would be the most calming colors for our brains? For example, some of the calming colors include blue (as the sky), green (as the grass), and brown (as the earth or sand). Consider this when deciding what color to paint a nursery for a newborn or an abode for your teenage son or daughter. It can make such a difference! The walls in our current home are all painted earth-tone colors (different shades of beige and brown), and we love it!

To remember the high-energy colors, look to signs for fast-food restaurants, like Kentucky Fried Chicken, McDonald's, or Pizza Hut, which are almost always painted red, orange, or deep yellow. Even the weather map is in sync. Red is indicative of the most intense part of the storm. As you move away from the intensity of the storm, the colors of the map move progressively toward calmer colors—yellows, greens, or blues. Nature even reflects the high-energy colors. Just look at the leaves changing in the fall. If you want a high-energy environment, go for those colors which will create it.

> How color affects the brain is influenced by our personalities and states of mind at the moment. A person who is very anxious and in a high state of stress may become more aggressive when seeing the color red, but if the person is relaxed, the same color red can trigger positive emotions (E. Jensen, 2008).

Music

Music has an unbelievable effect on the brain! It can make the hyperactive child less hyper and the angry child less angry. It has also been shown that the only time the entire cerebral cortex lights up in some autistic brains is when the person is listening to music. One grandparent related to me during a workshop that her grand-daughter was born with brain damage and her son and daughter-in-law were told that her grandchild would not be able to achieve certain milestones that other children her age would. Her parents believed in the power of music, so her father, who played the guitar, constantly sang to her, and her mother and father surrounded her with music. At the time she related the story, her granddaughter was attending kindergarten and had far exceeded any predictions made by her doctors. Never underestimate what the brain is capable of achieving! Music is even being played in recovery rooms follow-ing surgery to facilitate the healing process.

Music can literally change the state of the human brain. Television and movie directors already know this. How many times have you watched a movie with a heartbreaking plot, along with appropriate sentimental music, that moved you to tears? Conversely, you may have even been energized by the music of a movie. Consider the theme from the movie *Rocky* or the music played during a professional football or baseball game. No one will soon forget the music that accompanied the shark in the movie *Jaws*. After all, every time the music is heard, the shark also appears. It makes the shark more suspenseful! Let's consider the different states music can create in the brain.

The tempo, or beats per minute, of the music affects a child's breathing and heartbeat—two things that determine his or her mood or feelings (E. Jensen, 2009). Music with beats within the range of 50 to 70 per minute lines up with the human heart and calms the brain down. I know you have heard the saying, *Music soothes the savage breast.* Types of music within this range include, but are not limited to, classical (particularly from the baroque period), new age, smooth jazz, Celtic, Native American, and nature sounds. There are clocks currently developed so that people wake up to the calming sounds of nature such as water running over rocks or birds chirping rather than the annoying clamor of the typical alarm. The trouble is that the sounds are so soothing that many people sleep right through them!

Music with beats of approximately 110 to 160 per minute has a different effect. The body gets in tune with this faster pace and is energized and invigorated. People clap their hands or snap their fingers or rock to the beat. Music in this category includes most salsa music, rhythm and blues, rock and roll, or fast-paced country. By the way, here's a riddle. Do you know what you get

Music has the potential to increase muscular and molecular energy, influence the heartbeat, reduce pain and stress, speed up healing, relieve tiredness, and stimulate creativity and thinking (E. Jensen, 2008).

when you play a country song backwards? Give up? You get your wife back, you get your job back, you get your house back, and so forth.

My husband loves jazz, so you might hear that type of music played in our home at any time. I love all types of music, depending upon my mood, but my favorite concert pianist is Emile Pandolfi. Emile plays popular songs often from movies or Broadway shows, but he plays them as a classical pianist. He takes away my stress and places my brain in a state of euphoria. You will find titles of some of his recommended CDs in a subsequent section of this chapter.

Lighting

The worst possible light for the brain is fluorescent. Fluorescent light can not only make a child who is hyperactive more so, but it can cause the brains of those who are prone to epileptic seizures to seize. It can also make a migraine headache much worse. I know your next question: Then why are most schools replete with fluorescent lights? They happen to be the most cost-effective type of lighting, even if not the best. That's why!

The best possible light for the brain is, you guessed it, natural light or sunlight. There are places in the world that have 6 months of light and 6 months of darkness. During the 6 months of darkness, the incidences of depression, alcoholism, and suicide increase. There are chemicals that the sun helps the body produce that are naturally crucial to our mental and physical well-being. Lamplight at night, candlelight, and the alluring light from a fireplace also have the ability to calm and create positive states in our brains.

Your child's health and learning are influenced by lighting. Fluorescent lights possess a flicker and hum that can negatively impact the central nervous system by raising the levels of cortisol, or stress hormones (E. Jensen, 2008).

I asked our builder not to put any fluorescent lights in our home, not even in the kitchen. We have natural light from windows and recessed lighting in the ceiling. At night, we have a great deal of lamplight and, in the winter, the calming light of a fireplace.

To further illustrate the effects of these elements on the brain, compare the hustle-bustle atmosphere of a fast-food restaurant with that of an expensive dining experience. In the latter, the light source is often candlelight—so low, in fact, that you may have difficulty reading the menu. Look at the walls. They will probably be of an earth-tone color or deep green or maroon, but not loud. You may even hear a concert pianist playing your favorite calming songs. That is because the owners of the restaurant know what it will take to have you desire to return because of a pleasurable dining experience.

> In a study of 21,000 students in a tristate area, students whose classrooms had the most sunlight made 20% more progress on math tests and 26% more progress on reading tests than did their counterparts with less lighting (Heschong Mahone Consulting Group, 2007).

Aroma

Aromatherapy is big business! There are companies whose sole purpose is to create fragrances that cause your brain to act a certain way in public places such as department or grocery stores. Why do you think that some stores' bakery departments continue to bake bread throughout the day or realtors ask sellers to use fragrances to make their homes more appealing to potential buyers?

Calming aromas include lavender, vanilla, eucalyptus, and chamomile. These tend to relax the brain and create a state of well-being. High-energy aromas include citrus (particularly lemon or orange), cinnamon, and peppermint. These cause the brain to become more alert and create a state of anticipation. In one research study, even patients with brain injury performed as well as healthy patients in tests of vigilance following intermittent squirts of peppermint (Sullivan, Schefft, Warm, & Dember, 1998).

A word of caution is in order, however. Many children and adults have allergies. This would preclude the use of aromas in the home. You do not want to do anything that would aggravate an allergy. In our home, since none of us have allergies, I use a combination of plug-ins

> A person's sense of smell has uninterrupted, unfiltered access to the brain (E. Jensen, 2007).

and ceramic pots with liquid fragrance to create either relaxing or high-energy states in our brains. I also use aromatherapy in my car. On a long road trip, I can be relaxed or energized depending upon the fragrance in use.

Seating

When my children were in school, I prepared a well-lit spot in the house for studying and completing homework. It was a desk with a wooden chair that my oldest daughter, Jennifer, thought was the most uncomfortable spot in the entire house. She complained, yet I insisted that she sit there until she was finished. Needless to say, the homework was completed in record time. Years later, after delving into the brain research, I altered my decision. I made a deal with Jennifer. I told her that if she could complete her homework successfully, she could choose where she sat as she did it. We were both happier, and Jenny stuck to her part of the bargain. The homework was well done!

Many children need alternative forms of seating while they are studying. Some may even need to take frequent breaks or stand up for a while. See Chapter 16 in this book for research on the strong correlation between movement and long-term memory. After reading this chapter, you may even want to stand when you attempt to recall content from your workplace. After all, most jobs in the real world require that adults be active participants in the jobs to which they are assigned. Even if you have a desk job, your boss probably does not stand over you forbidding you from getting up from your desk when need be.

HOW CAN I MAKE IT HAPPEN?

○ Be mindful of the effect of color on the brain when you decide what color to paint your newborn's nursery or your child's room. Calming colors for them will more likely be pastels, such as light blues or greens, or earth tones (beiges and browns). For a high-energy nursery or child's room, walls painted the colors of red, orange, or deep yellow will suffice. Just keep in mind the fact that your child needs to play and sleep in the same room.

○ When you are working with your children and you need to write something, write with a blue marker. Things that you need to bring to the attention of your children, such as punctuation or important vocabulary, should probably be written in red. Research has shown that underlining key concepts and important words with colored markers tends to improve memory and visual recognition (E. Jensen & Dabney, 2000).

○ When you want your children to unwind or relax, play calming music. Even on a long road trip, play calming music in the car. Watch the arguments and the annoying questions from your children, such as *When are we going to be there?*, turn to relaxation, rest, or even sleep. classical, new age, Celtic, and Native American music are just a few of the types you may want to get. Some of my favorite CDs by calming concert pianist Emile Pandolfi include *By Request*, *An Affair to Remember*, and *The Days of Wine and Roses*. His CDs are easy to find if you access them online.

○ As your children complete homework, such as solving math problems or outlining a science chapter, have calming music playing softly in the background. If they are trying to memorize something and the music is distracting, then refrain from using it.

○ When completing an arduous task such as cleaning the house or washing the car, put on high-energy music and have your children complete the task while listening to it. Bodies tend to get in sync with the music played around them. High-energy music such as rock and roll, salsa, rhythm and blues, positive rap, or fast-paced country-western will get the heads nodding and the toes tapping, and the task will be completed much more easily.

○ Fluorescent lights provide the worst possible light for brains for the reasons mentioned in the introduction of this chapter. Most homes only have them in the kitchen, but if your home has them in other places, you may want to turn off some or all of them. Lower lights appear to create calm; however, be sure that if your children are reading or doing homework, the light is sufficient for achieving the tasks.

○ Some children are getting such limited amounts of vitamin D that doctors are beginning to recommend that children take supplements. One of the best sources of vitamin D is the sun. Natural sunlight positively affects the brain's and body's concentration, energy levels, and moods, which also impact learning. Take your children outdoors for play or a walk and allow the sun to help your bodies manufacture vitamin D. Even doing it twice a week will help.

○ Check Bed, Bath and Beyond, Yankee Candle, or other similar stores and sample the aromas that strike your fancy. What one person likes, another does not. Place your favorite scents in strategic places in your home or car and watch the state of your family's brains change accordingly. Use lavender, vanilla, eucalyptus, or chamomile to calm the brain and citrus (particularly lemon or orange), peppermint, or cinnamon to influence mood and attention and help the brain become more alert. I like to smell the orange aroma when I am writing. It enables me to think! Be cautious about the fact that many children and adults have allergies. Don't use aromatherapy if it would do anything to activate the allergies of anyone in the family.

○ The attention span of your children is approximately equal to their age in minutes (Feinstein, 2009). Therefore, the attention span of your 10-year-old is approximately 10 minutes, for your 16-year-old, 16 minutes. Here is the bad news: for an 85-year-old, the attention span is not 85 minutes! The longest time even the adult brain can pay conscious attention is approximately 20 minutes. Allow your children to take short breaks if the time devoted to homework becomes too long and they become restless. However, that theory can be discarded if students are engaged, entertained, or having fun. This is the reason that children can sit through a 2-hour movie or play video games nonstop.

ACTION PLAN

> What will I commit to do to ensure that my child(ren)
> are surrounded with a calming environment?

What am I already doing that I should continue to do?

1. _____
   _____
   _____.

2. _____
   _____
   _____.

3. _____
   _____
   _____.

4. _____
   _____
   _____.

What new habits will I commit to developing?

1. _____
   _____
   _____.

2. _____
   _____
   _____.

3. _____
   _____
   _____.

4. _____
   _____
   _____.

Give Your Child a Brain-Healthy Start

Begin with the end in mind.

—Covey, 2004

WHAT DOES THAT MEAN?

Success in school and in life does not begin at birth. It begins before birth. Prospective parents must give their offspring the best chance of growing up healthy and happy, and research tells us that certain practices give the brain the opportunity to accomplish this goal. In fact, the effects of diet can influence a person's brain activity ranging anywhere from 10% to 65% (E. Jensen, 2007). Let's examine the effects of some of the following positive practices not only for initial health but for continued long life as well.

Encourage Proper Nutrition and Hydration

For the first time in 200 years, American children may have a life expectancy that is shorter than that of their parents (Colbert, 2009). Why? One reason is obesity! Children are simply overeating or not eating the right things that are necessary for proper brain and body development. The brain is a very demanding organ. It comprises only 2% of the total body weight, but consumes 8 to 10 times more oxygen and glucose than any other organ in the body. Since the brain does not have the capacity to store energy for later use like the liver or the muscles, if the body does not receive the needed nutrition, the brain is the first to suffer, and learning and memory are compromised (Markowitz & Jensen, 2007).

A report in the *New England Journal of Medicine* predicts that the rise in childhood obesity could reduce the lifespan of the current generation by 5 years (Colbert, 2009).

As a rule of thumb, when you think about nutrition, it is best to eat a meal that consists of lean protein, a small amount of fat, some carbohydrates, and, as a whole, a very moderate amount of calories. It is further recommended that the proteins be eaten before the carbohydrates; If you do the opposite, the brain and body may become sluggish.

Organic foods are those that have been produced without the use of chemical fertilizers or artificial pesticides and can be identified by looking for the USDA *organic* label. When organic foods are either not available or too expensive, remember the following rules: (1) The thicker the peel, the safer the fruit. Bananas, oranges, lemons, grapefruit, and watermelons are examples of fruits with thick peels; (2) look for organic varieties of foods with thin or no peels such as apples, celery, peaches, lettuce, or broccoli; (3) thoroughly wash produce prior to cooking with a natural biodegradable cleanser or detergent; and (4) soak produce in a sink of cold water to which you have added one tablespoon of 35% food-grade hydrogen peroxide for 5 to 15 minutes. Then rinse thoroughly with fresh water (Colbert, 2009).

Not only are children eating inappropriately, but they are eating and sitting. Many years ago, when people did not eat as they should, they had the advantage of working off the food through manual labor. Now, children are sitting in front of televisions, video games, and computers. In fact, the only thing that some are exercising is their thumbs while sending text messages. The result is childhood obesity and a higher incidence of type 2 diabetes than ever before.

The brain and body also need appropriate hydration. In fact, when the body is 3% dehydrated, the brain is 30% dehydrated. When people experience joint pain, heartburn, or even depression, their bodies are often expressing the need for water. Children who do not drink enough water may have dehydrated brains that could become restless or lethargic or give up on academic tasks (E. Jensen, 2007).

But how much water is too much? You might be surprised! If you take your weight and divide it by two, you will get the number of ounces of water you should drink each day (Colbert, 2009). But do not dismay! Water does not have to be consumed only in liquid form. You will normally get a quart of water per day just by eating lots of vegetables and fruits. For example, lettuce and watermelons are more than 90% water and a banana is 70% water.

Avoid Alcohol and Drugs

Thanks to the blood–brain barrier, a built-in straining mechanism for the brain, most bodies can handle a moderate level of toxins. Too many toxins and your body's immune system suffers. Drugs, whether prescription or not, alcohol, and nicotine from cigarettes are all potentially toxic for your body (Markowitz & Jensen, 2007).

From the moment my daughter Jennifer and daughter-in-law, Amanda, knew that they were pregnant, I advised them to eliminate any over-the-counter drugs and all wine from their diets. Since we do not know for sure how drugs and alcohol affect the growing fetal brain and much of the brain development occurs during the first trimester, it is better to avoid them at all costs. According to Markowitz & Jensen (2007), the National Institute on Alcohol Abuse and Alcoholism claims that even very low doses of alcohol can inhibit the ability of various memory cells in the brain to function.

Jennifer is a teacher, and several years ago, she had a beautiful little girl in her second grade class whose mother was addicted to cocaine when she was born. While we do not know for sure whether the cocaine addiction attributed to this child's erratic behavior, we do know that not only did this child have severe learning difficulties, but she was also prone to violent outbursts and often had to be restrained.

While the jury is still out on the long-term effects of caffeine intake, we know that caffeine may stimulate the brain, but it also decreases blood flow simultaneously, which is why coffee is used in the treatment of migraine headaches. As miraculous as the brain is, it stands a much better chance of developing normally when not

Studies have shown that the brains of humans who drink heavily tend to weigh less and their frontal lobes contain smaller and fewer neurons than do those of nondrinkers (Markowitz & Jensen, 2007).

impacted by the toxic environments that drugs, alcohol, and nicotine use can create.

HOW CAN I MAKE IT HAPPEN?

○ Give your baby the best chance for healthy brain and body development by seeing a doctor as soon as you know you are pregnant and following that doctor's orders during pregnancy. Be sure to eat healthy, supplement with vitamins, and refrain from any drugs (over-the-counter or otherwise) and alcohol use while pregnant. In schools, we are experiencing the effects of children whose parents were taking drugs and consuming alcohol while expecting. Severe abnormalities in learning and behavior are resulting.

○ Four crucial elements for healthy brain and body development include eating fresh fruits and vegetables, drinking lots of pure water, controlling the amount of salt, sugar, and fat we take in, and limiting the preservatives, additives, and chemically treated food we eat (Markowitz & Jensen, 2007). The following foods are recommended as optimal for healthy brain development not only during pregnancy but throughout life. As you shop for groceries and prepare dinner, consider including some of these on your menu.

Fresh Vegetables (2–3 servings daily)	Omega-3-Rich Proteins (2–3 servings daily)	Fruits (2–3 servings daily)	Carbohydrates (1–3 servings daily)	Beverages (8–12 servings daily)
Broccoli Peas Carrots Leafy greens Potatoes	Chicken Turkey Tuna Salmon Eggs Yogurt Organ meats Sardines Anchovies Mackerel Shellfish Soybeans	Bananas Avocados Blueberries Oranges Strawberries Tomatoes	Whole grains Beans Sunflower seeds Nuts	Pure water Green tea Fresh fruit juice

(Markowitz & Jensen, 2007, p. 109)

○ Have your children accompany you to the store and assist you in shopping for the groceries for dinner. Let them help you select vegetables, fruits, and other categories of food. Then allow them to assist you in preparing the actual dinner. Children will be more likely to eat what they themselves select and cook for a meal.

○ Allow your children to see you eating healthier. Choose and prepare beverages and foods with very little added sugar, artificial sweetener, or salt; avoid saturated and trans fats; and select foods dense in nutrients and rich in vitamins and minerals with very few calories (Parent Educational Tools, 2008). Remember it is not what you say to your children but what they see you actually doing that makes an impression on their day-to-day practices. Sit down and eat a healthy meal together. Drink water together throughout the day.

○ Since breakfast is the most important meal of the day, provide a healthy breakfast for your children to get their day off to a most advantageous start. The breakfast can be as simple as a muffin or bowl of whole grain cereal, fresh fruit or fruit juice, and yogurt. If you are unable to make breakfast for your children, have them take advantage of the breakfast programs provided by some school systems throughout the country.

○ Limit the number of times per month that you and your children eat food from fast-food restaurants. It is very tempting to drive by McDonald's or Kentucky Fried Chicken since time is of the essence when you are on your way to soccer practice or ballet. However, when you do go to these places, help your children select healthier foods from their menus.

○ Limit the amount of time your children spend daily in sedentary activities such as watching television, playing video games, working on the computer (including Internet activities), or talking on the cell phone or text messaging. Set a schedule of how much time can be spent daily in these activities and have your children stick to that schedule.

○ Get your children moving. Engage them in physical activities that will assist their bodies in burning calories, and do it together, since it will be good for all family members. This is the reason the National Football League has initiated Play60, encouraging children to spend 60 minutes engaged in physical activity daily. Recently, the Atlanta Falcons football team broke the

Guinness Book of World Records record by assembling the largest number of children on a football field to exercise simultaneously.

○ Since going without protein can reduce mental functioning, select a variety of lean foods from the protein group every week such as fish, dry peas and beans, seeds and nuts, meats, poultry, and eggs and include them in the menu for you and your children.

○ Encourage your children to drink water consistently throughout the day in lieu of sugary drinks. Their brains and bodies will thank you. Provide water while students are completing their homework for proper hydration. Remember to take their weight and divide it by two as a guide to determine the number of ounces of liquid they should have per day. Don't forget that some of this liquid will come from the fruits and vegetables they consume.

○ Encourage your children to eat generous servings of fresh fruits and vegetables daily. Not only will this practice go far in ensuring that their bodies acquire necessary amounts of water, but a healthier body also becomes the order of the day.

○ Free radicals are atoms in the body that are not paired with electrons, so they steal electrons from other atoms. This causes a chain reaction of cell damage. Simply breathing can produce free radicals. However, diseases like cancers, coronary artery disease, Alzheimer's, and multiple sclerosis, as well as some recurring colds, bronchitis, and bladder infections, can create additional free radicals. Antioxidants keep free radicals under control since they have the ability to neutralize them. Therefore, eating foods rich in antioxidants will create a healthier family. Some of the best foods rich in antioxidants include blueberries; blackberries; cranberries; strawberries; raspberries; red kidney, pinto, and dried black beans; artichokes; prunes; pecans; apples; cherries; plums; and cooked potatoes (Colbert, 2009).

ACTION PLAN

What will I commit to do to ensure that my child(ren)
get a brain-healthy start in life?

What am I already doing that I should continue to do?

1. _____
   _____
   _____.

2. _____
   _____
   _____.

3. _____
   _____
   _____.

4. _____
   _____
   _____.

What new habits will I commit to developing?

1. _____
   _____
   _____.

2. _____
   _____
   _____.

3. _____
   _____
   _____.

4. _____
   _____
   _____.

Talk To and With Your Child

The earliest conversations between a parent and a child are the beginning of that child's emotional, social, and academic life.

—Wingert & Brant, 2005

WHAT DOES THAT MEAN?

My husband, Tyrone, and I were in a hotel in New York City several years ago when I saw something that I had hoped never to see. We were in the hotel lobby in Manhattan when I spotted a double stroller. In the stroller were two adorable children who looked to be about 2 and 4 years old. Built into each section of the double stroller was a DVD player. Both children were watching different videos as their mother was pushing them around the lobby. I commented to Tyrone how wonderful it would have been if both children had been paying attention to the smells, sights, and sounds of New York City rather than watching separate movies. The experience would have been so much more enriching and their brains would have greatly benefited.

Due to advances in modern technology, images are coming into the brains of all of us faster than ever before, and it is shortening all of our attention spans. How many of you get impatient when your computer does not immediately do exactly as you want? Yet that technology should never replace the time that parents spend in meaningful conversation with their children. That conversation should begin before birth and continue throughout their lives. Years ago, much of that conversation went on at the dinner table when families sat down daily and talked about life. With our busy lifestyles today, families seldom sit together for a meal, yet the importance of that time has not decreased at all.

Much of the conversation that went on with my children as they were growing up took place in the car as we were traveling to extracurricular activities: soccer, baseball, piano lessons, and ballet. We turned off the radio and we talked in the car. If you have established a good relationship with your children from birth, then this conversation comes more naturally. Now, children are so busy watching DVDs in the car or listening to their iPods that family talk is at a premium. With all the technological innovations, such as television, iPods, video games, DVDs, text messages, and computers, I am convinced that it is possible to give birth to a child and not have to talk with them at all! But here is the problem. The need for human interaction is one of the basic needs of the brain. Why do you think so many teenagers are on the Internet talking to strangers? The danger is that they may be talking to people with whom you would rather they not associate.

You may wonder about the effects of television on the brain. It is recommended by the American Academy of Pediatrics (Nemours, 2007) that young children under the age of 2 not look at television at all and that viewing time be limited for older preschool children to 1 to 2 hours daily of quality programming (Nemours Foundation, 2007). Viewing television does not properly stimulate the visual system of the brain since there

> A well-developed and strong ability to connect with the world, especially their parents, is extremely important when babies begin making their earliest efforts at learning to speak (Wingert & Brant, 2005).

> Since words are crucial in building the thought connections in the brain, the more language a child encounters through conversation with other people, as well as through books, the larger advantage they will have socially and educationally for the rest of their lives (Fox, 2001).

is no dilation of the pupils, the eyes do not move from one point to the next like what happens when one reads, the images change too fast to be processed by the higher-thinking areas of the brain, and the child's brain is not allowed to create internal images (Sousa, 2007). The act of viewing television is passive and does not enable children to talk back. It is that talking back, or two-way conversation, that is crucial to making connections in the brain.

Let me tell you a funny story! My granddaughter, Aidan, is a very verbal child. This did not happen by accident. My daughter Jennifer and her husband, Lex, talk to Aidan constantly and have done so since before she was born. Several months ago, when Aidan was 20 months old, she happened to be doing something that she should not have been. Jennifer told Aidan that by the time she counted to three, the behavior should stop. Jennifer said, *One!* Aidan said, *Two!* Jen had to work hard to keep from laughing. She soon found out that at 20 months, Aidan could easily count to 10, not only in English but in Spanish and Chinese as well. Why? Jennifer had counted things in the real world with Aidan numerous times. They counted as they went up the steps. They counted the toys in Aidan's room. They counted everything.

Children learn their first language through the auditory cortex, which receives feedback by listening to other people and to their own speech. Birds even learn to sing by listening to adult birds (Rodriguez, 2007). The earliest conversations between a parent and a child are the beginning of that child's emotional, social, and academic

> The more often children are talked to, the more they will understand. *From listening comes speaking, and from speaking comes reading* (Sprenger, 2008b).

life (Wingert & Brant, 2005). In fact, unless a child reaches a minimal level of competence with social skills by the age of 6, the child is at risk for the remainder of his or her life (Dowling, 2005). Limit the time your children spend interacting with technology and allow them to interact with you. Their brains will thank you!

HOW CAN I MAKE IT HAPPEN?

○ There is evidence to suggest that a fetus's hearing is so acute that as early as the sixth or seventh month in the womb, a child is able to tell the difference between a positive or soothing voice and a negative or disturbing voice (Trelease, 2001). Infants even turn to their parents' voices when they are only hours old. I was fortunate to be in the delivery room when my granddaughter, Aidan, was born. She came out crying but immediately turned in the direction of her father's voice when he called her name. It was as if she heard a voice that she already knew. She did already know that voice since he had talked to her throughout the 9 months of Jennifer's pregnancy. Talk to your child before he or she is born.

○   Parents need to have loving, laughing, deep, and meaningful conversations with their kids long before the age of 3 since children can't learn to talk unless they are spoken to (Fox, 2001). Talk with your child face to face. Smile! Talk slowly but in complete sentences. You would be surprised how much vocabulary children experience when their parents encourage conversation.

○   Make a trip to the grocery store or another location an educational experience. Point out and name the groceries on the shelf. Talk about the colors of the boxes or bags. Count the number of items on the shelf. Discuss categories of merchandise such as vegetables, fruits, juices, meats, or poultry.

○   When giving children verbal directions, remember that the number of directions a child can retain is correlated to age. From birth to age 3, one direction at a time is appropriate, such as *Go and get your red sweater.* A 4- or 5-year-old should be able to hold two directions; a 6- or 7-year-old, three directions; an 8 or 9-year-old, four directions. The number increases every other year up to seven directions from age 15 to adult. It may not be coincidental that so many lists in the adult world come in sevens—days of the week, notes on the scale, colors in the rainbow, continents, dwarfs, and *Habits of Highly Effective People.*

○   Do not use television as a babysitter. Children below the age of 2 should probably not be looking at television at all. TV time for older children should be limited. Sit with your child and select the shows that are appropriate to watch and watch with your child. So many shows today can have a negative effect on the brains of your children due to the increased violence, profanity, and sexual content.

○   By 1 year of age, children have learned all the sounds that comprise the native language that they will speak. That is why people have difficulty speaking languages learned later in life with perfect accents (Fox, 2001). Introduce your children to a second language early. I often present in countries where people speak two, three, four, or more languages. I ask them at what age they learned so many languages and the answer is usually *When*

I was little! Yet in the United States, even though many of us took foreign language classes in middle or high school, 80% of people fail to speak a second language as a native speaker. Perhaps we are waiting too late to acquire the second language!

○ When traveling in the car, turn off the radio and the DVD player. Have your children take the ear buds out of their ears and cease the text messaging. Engage your children in conversation. Ask them about their school day and tell them about your day. Talk about their wants and desires and their short- and long-term goals, and share yours. It will make a difference in your relationship with your children. See Chapter 1 for additional ways to develop a relationship with children of any age.

○ Both parents should talk with their children daily, but set aside a time each week just to sit and have a meaningful conversation. It is important that both parents are present for the conversation, not just mom or dad. If you have more than one child, try to set a different time for each one. Remember you have two ears and one mouth for a reason. You should listen to what they have to say much more than you should offer advice to them. This time can go a long way in showing your interest in what is happening personally to your children.

○ Make your children aware that when they have a problem, they can come to you and talk about it. Habit 5 of *The 7 Habits of Highly Effective People* is *Seek first to understand, then to be understood* (Covey, 2004). Listen to what they have to say and then help them to problem solve the situation. Questions that could be included in the conversation are the following: (1) Describe what happened. (2) How did you respond? (3) Do you think that your response was appropriate? (4) If the same situation were to happen again, would you respond differently?

○ Encourage your children to practice their social skills through the use of conversation with you, other adults, and their friends. In fact, social intelligence appears to make people more successful in the real world than does general intelligence (Goleman, 1995). Children today are so accustomed to text messaging and e-mailing that they appear to be losing the art of social interaction. When I go into classrooms to teach, I am amazed at the number of students who cannot look me in the eye, shake my hand, and say *Good morning!* Yet when asked, CEOs of major corporations will tell you that interpersonal skills are still highly valued in the workplace. Those skills need to be cultivated early and can help make your child very successful throughout life.

ACTION PLAN

What will I commit to do to ensure that I spend
time talking with my child(ren)?

What am I already doing that I should continue to do?

1. _____
_____
_____.

2. _____
_____
_____.

3. _____
_____
_____.

4. _____
_____
_____.

What new habits will I commit to developing?

1. _____
_____
_____.

2. _____
_____
_____.

3. _____
_____
_____.

4. _____
_____
_____.

Read To and With Your Child

The fire of literacy is created by the emotional relationship between a child, a book, and the person reading it aloud.

—Fox, 2001

WHAT DOES THAT MEAN?

If you are accustomed to reading the same book aloud to your children and/or grandchildren over and over again, you will know that if you attempt to skip a page, not only do children know it, but they will make you go back and reread the story correctly. Let me recommend a wonderful book by Geoffrey Kloske and Barry Blitt (2005) called *Once Upon a Time, the End: Asleep in 60 Seconds*. It is the story of a father who is so tired of reading the same story every single night to his child that he begins to shorten or summarize the story so that it can be read in less than a minute. The book contains many fairy tales and nursery rhymes that can be read in less than 60 seconds. While it is an excellent book for teaching summarizing, it is also hilarious and should be enjoyed by all parents. For example, in the book, the fairy tale *Goldilocks and the Bears* is shortened to the following summary:

Goldilocks and the Bears

There were some bears,

It really doesn't matter how many.

There was a bunch.

Let's get to the point:

While they were out, a blonde girl

Ate a bear's porridge,

Broke a bear's chair,

And fell asleep in a bear's bed.

When the bears came back,

They found her asleep.

She woke up, screamed, and ran home

So she could sleep in her own bed.

Just like you.

The end.

As I work in schools today, I find that many children do not know fairy tales or nursery rhymes, simply because no one has read them aloud. Yet the colorful pictures, exciting sounds, and the rhymes of *Mother Goose* have lasted for generations. When these nursery rhymes are sung or recited, both rhyme and activity in your children's mind are reinforced. Since many fairy tales do not come with pictures, another benefit of reading them aloud is that children's brains have to work harder visualizing their own pictures.

Albert Einstein, one of the most brilliant men in history, tells the story of a time when he recommended fairy tales to a woman who wanted the answer to how to make her son more intelligent. Einstein told the woman that fairy stories would help her child's brain pay attention to detail, problem solve, predict, make meaning, and experience emotion. Smart man! As children learn to read, it is also vital that they develop the ability to hear rhymes and alliterations and play with speech sounds (Tallal, 2007).

Children who are read to from birth quickly acquire the ability to listen, concentrate, relax, and await the desire to hear stories that give them immense pleasure (Fox, 2001). When a parent is reading to a child, the child can also see that the parent is reading from left to right and modeling enthusiasm for fluency, reading, and intonation (Sprenger, 2008). This modeling will help the child acquire the same left-to-right and fluency behaviors when they begin to read themselves.

Recently I was browsing in a bookstore near my home when I came upon a beautiful sight—a mother sitting on the floor in the children's section of the bookstore with her son on her lap reading a picture book aloud to him. I just stopped and smiled. I could tell that this was not the child's first time being read to, since he was paying rapt attention to his mother's voice and the beautiful pictures in the story. As children experience being read to numerous times, they will want to imitate the act by reading aloud themselves.

> Between the ages of 7 and 8, many children begin to read fluently with the ability to decode words they do not know and break them into syllables (Shaywitz, 2003).

According to Jim Trelease (2001) a noted educator and author of the time-tested *The Read-Aloud Handbook*, the following four factors appear to be present in the home environment of almost every early reader: (1) The child is read to regularly and his or her parents are avid readers; (2) a wide variety of printed materials are in the home; (3) paper and pencil are available so that children can scribble and draw; and (4) family members stimulate the child's interest in reading and writing by answering countless questions, buying books, taking the child to the library, displaying the child's work, and writing stories that the child dictates.

Now try this personal visualization. Picture yourself sitting in a cozy chair or on a sofa with your child snuggled up close to you or visualize yourself sitting next to or lying on a bed with your child tucked securely in while you read a variety of stories. You are even using various types of voices and many sound effects as you read aloud. The result can be unforgettable time together and a life-long love of reading and books for the two of you. When this happens, the benefits for you and your child are immeasurable!

HOW CAN I MAKE IT HAPPEN?

Begin reading aloud from the day you bring your children home from the hospital so that they get in the habit while they are still young enough to want to imitate what they are seeing and hearing. If the child is old enough to be talked to at birth, the child is old enough to

Language milestones are commensurate with the development and maturation of the language areas in the brain (Eliot, 2007).

be read to as well. There are many advantages to this practice. When a parent is reading to a child, the connections in a parent's brain begin to take place in the child's brain (Restak, 2001). According to Mem Fox (2001), *the first day of school is almost too late for a child to begin to learn to read.* In fact, children need to have had about 1,000 stories read to them before they will be able to read themselves. That is one of the reasons that a parent is a child's best and first teacher.

o Never use the excuse that you don't have time to read aloud to your children. People tend to find time for the things that they value. Value this practice. Eliminate some television time or put some chores aside so that you can spend quality time reading aloud to your children. It will be well worth the time spent! Whether a child becomes a proficient reader is dependent not only on genetic factors but also on the environment in which the child is raised (Nevills & Wolfe, 2009).

o When reading aloud to children, keep the length of the reading time in line with their attention spans. Remember that a child's attention span in minutes is approximately equal to her or his age. Therefore, you might initially read aloud for 5 minutes to a 5-year-old, 10 minutes to a 10-year-old, and 12 minutes to a 12-year-old. Gradually lengthen the time spent reading aloud as children get accustomed to the act or as they show continued interest. When the brain is enjoying what it is doing, attention span is considerably lengthened. Be sure that the read-alouds are exciting and interesting enough to maintain your children's attention while you are simultaneously increasing their imaginations.

o Take your children to the public library and get them a library card so that they will realize the importance of books. When they are old enough, have them select their own books for reading aloud and, eventually, have them select books that they can read aloud to you.

o Give books as gifts for your children and for other special people in your life. In this way, you will model your value for reading as a life-long practice. It is particularly impressive when children see their fathers reading as well as their mothers so that they realize that the act of reading is vital to every person in the family.

o To determine if a book you are planning to check out of the library or buy is appropriate for your child to read aloud to you, try the five-finger test. Open the book near the front and have your child read approximately 100 words aloud. Every time your child misses a word, secretly put up one finger. When you have put up five fingers, the passage may be too difficult. Try a 100-word passage near the middle and another one near the end of the book using the same test. If your child misses many more than five words in two of the three 100-word passages, the book may be too difficult for now. You may still check out the book, but use it as a read-aloud.

○ Once your children have learned to read, use the *PPP* technique when taking turns reading aloud. *PPP* stands for page, paragraph, or pass. When reading with you, your children can elect to read an entire page of the book, one paragraph, or pass their turn to you. You can elect to do the same.

○ Have books at your disposal so that wherever you or your children are waiting, such as in the doctor's or dentist's offices, or during a plane or bus ride, your time can be occupied in the best way possible: reading together.

○ Give your children the essentials of *encouragement, time, books, magazines, light, silence, warmth in winter and coolness in summer, and the comfort of being allowed to read in bed every night* (Fox, 2001).

○ A fun activity that helps your children develop fluency is to engage them in a game of repeated readings. Let your child select several pages from a book that he or she can read alone. Buy a kitchen timer and set it for a certain amount of time, such as 1 or 2 minutes. Have your child begin reading as you set the timer and read aloud until the time is up. If your child does not know a word in the passage, say the word and allow him or her to keep reading. When the time is up, have your child count the number of words read in the allotted time. Then have him or her reread the same passage for the same amount of time for the purpose of reading more words. Count the words again, which hopefully will be higher. You may even want to repeat it a third time. Then use the same procedure on another day with a different passage. This technique can provide practice in oral reading and helps your child to develop fluency.

○ As your children get older, add an occasional family reading time. Turn off the television and read together, with every family member reading her or his own book or taking turns reading a book that the entire family can enjoy. If your children see you making time to read, you will be modeling a life-long love of reading that does not stop once a person has completed formal schooling.

ACTION PLAN

What will I commit to do to ensure that my child(ren)
are being read to or are reading daily?

What am I already doing that I should continue to do?

1. _____
   _____
   _____.

2. _____
   _____
   _____.

3. _____
   _____
   _____.

4. _____
   _____
   _____.

What new habits will I commit to developing?

1. _____
   _____
   _____.

2. _____
   _____
   _____.

3. _____
   _____
   _____.

4. _____
   _____
   _____.

Provide Opportunities for Creative Play

Play is seen in some studies as an essential protein in a child's emotional diet.

—Gibbs, 2009

WHAT DOES THAT MEAN?

Remember when you were little and you went outdoors or you stayed indoors, but you played. I mean, truly played! From the age of 6, I knew that I wanted to be a teacher. I would pretend that my dolls were my students and teach them in my bedroom for hours on end. Amazingly, I had no discipline problems! My Chatty Cathy would not even talk unless I pulled her string! Younger parents are wondering what a Chatty Cathy is. For those who do not know, it was a doll that you could make talk by pulling the string in the back of her neck.

With play when we were little, certain things happened, even if we were not aware of them. We learned to share our toys; we learned to resolve conflict; and we learned to become creative and imaginative as we pretended that we were not ourselves, but a princess or an astronaut or a teacher. When children are allowed to play with other children, they learn formal rules as well as the informal rules of cooperation, negotiation, camaraderie, and physical skills (E. Jensen, 2007). Play helps children experience empathy and determine what course of action to take in any given situation.

Yet from 1981 to 1997, there was a 25% decrease in time for free play for 6- to 8-year-olds while homework more than doubled (Gibbs, 2009). Oftentimes, the brain is not allowed to rest between learning segments, and brain chemicals, called neurotransmitters, become depleted. Because of this, it becomes frustrating and much more difficult for the child to make connections from one neuron to the next neuron (Willis, 2006). By the way, play has been found to be not just for the young. The ability to play games is one of the 10 things that keep people living beyond the age of 80 (Mahoney, 2005). The saying is *You don't stop playing because you grow old, you grow old because you stop playing.* Therefore, whether you are 8 or 80, it appears that you should be playing.

Much of the play for students today appears to be technological. While there are advantages to this type of play, there are also disadvantages. With outdoor and active play, imagination and creativity increase. We were also better able to visualize. With technological play, vivid, colorful images are the order of the day. Why does the brain need to imagine in a video game or on the computer when everything is already there, and in living color no less?

Another advantage to creative play is the physical movement it requires. The American Academy of Pediatrics warns that health risks can result with a decrease in playtime, including increased stress and anxiety and an explosion of childhood obesity (Gibbs, 2009). The sedentary lifestyle, or lack of exercise, that many children experience when playing video games or watching television has resulted in an increase in type 2 diabetes.

Even in the school setting, recess is essential. Some researchers believe that a child's physical and motor skills may be hardwired in the brain, rather than learned, and that age 5 may be the end of the period for optimal growth in those areas (Bergen, 2006).

Children who were not allowed playtime at school had trouble sitting still, were unable to focus, and developed ADHD symptoms (Sunderland, 2006).

When children are playing outdoors, another side benefit is the vitamin D derived from the sun. Research also indicates that 20% of children and adults younger than 50 and 95% of adults over 50 have an inadequate intake of the vitamin D, which the sun provides (Colbert, 2009). This vitamin D is crucial for normal bone and tooth development and may protect adults from breast and prostate cancer and prevent multiple sclerosis.

HOW CAN I MAKE IT HAPPEN?

○ Provide time for your children to play outdoors. Accompany them to the park or another outdoor location and allow them to interact with other children, slide down the sliding board, or ride the merry-go-round. Not only will posi-

> When children play together, they learn how to handle social interactions and relationships and how to recognize their own and others' emotions (Goleman, 1995).

tive brain chemicals be produced, but life skills will also be developed and imagination increased.

○ Turn off the television and computer and take the family outdoors. Engage your children in a game of catch, throw the Frisbee, conduct relay races, ride bikes, or play touch football. In other words, just have fun soaking up the vitamin D from the sun and actively playing with your children. I still have memories of my sisters and I playing straight-base baseball in the backyard when I was growing up.

○ Provide your child with some *downtime*, time when they are not being hurried here or there or engaged in other activities. After all, some of the most creative thoughts occur when the brain has time to think, invent its own game, or create its own ways to entertain itself.

○ Experience some fun! Have your children stand up and use their elbow to *write* their first name, their other elbow to *write* their middle name, and their hip to *write* their last name, their other hip to *write* their best friend's name, and their head to *write* your name (E. Jensen, 2007). Not only will this activity enable the body parts involved to move, but it also puts the names in one of the strongest memory systems in the brain, *procedural* or *muscle memory*. We will discuss this concept further in Chapter 16.

○ Let your children lead you in a series of stretches. Allow them to select the music, either fast- or slow-paced, and have your children decide whether the stretches will be slow and relaxing or calisthenics (E. Jensen, 2007).

○ Although swings, merry-go-rounds, and sliding boards are difficult to find on playgrounds today, the acts of swinging and rocking develop the inner ear, balance, and your children's reading skills as well as stimulate the vestibular system. Take advantage of these pieces of equipment when you find them (E. Jensen, 2007).

○ Clap, stomp, or skip out a rhythm or pattern and then have your children repeat the pattern that you clap, stomp, or skip. Start with simple patterns and then, as your children get better, increase the difficulty of the pattern.

○ Spinning the body develops the brain. Play high-energy, upbeat music and allow your children to spin in a circle twice a day for 1 minute in each direction. Have them close their eyes and then spin in one direction and then the other. Closing the eyes will minimize the dizziness and help them practice orienting themselves (E. Jensen, 2007).

○ Engage your children in activities that force them to cross the midline of the body and improve visual tracking. An example would be the windmill, where children stand with their feet apart and their arms reaching out to the sides. Have your children swing their right hand down to touch their left toe while keeping the legs straight. Then have them swing the left hand down to the right toe and continue alternating at different speeds. When the midline of the body is crossed, the hemispheres of the brain are lateralized and learning is improved (Lengel & Kuczala, 2010).

○ Have your children practice walking a line or balance beam, since this activity improves spatial skills and reading ability. Have them walk at least 3 meters along a line taped on the floor or along a long piece of wood placed on the ground. Make the game more challenging by having them walk the line with closed eyes.

○ Have the whole family play triangle tag. Have three family members hold hands and run in a circle while a fourth family member tries to tag a designated group member. The spinning group continually turns and changes directions to avoid the tag (E. Jensen, 2007).

○ Have your children participate in vigorous physical activity each day; the American Heart Association and the National Football League suggest that all children and adolescents actively participate in a minimum of 60 minutes of moderate to vigorous physical activity daily (Parent Educational Tools, 2008).

ACTION PLAN

What will I commit to do to ensure that my child(ren) have opportunities for creative play?

What am I already doing that I should continue to do?

1. _____
_____
_____.

2. _____
_____
_____.

3. _____
_____
_____.

4. _____
_____
_____.

What new habits will I commit to developing?

1. _____
_____
_____.

2. _____
_____
_____.

3. _____
_____
_____.

4. _____
_____
_____.

Teach Your Child Rules, Rituals, and Responsibility

Parenting style has a great impact on what kind of adult a child turns out to be.

—Wingert & Brant, 2005

WHAT DOES THAT MEAN?

There appears to be a recent movement among many parents that childhood should be a carefree and joyful time and that their children are happier when all rules and responsibilities are taken away. Nothing could be further from the truth. If you read the research (Runkel, 2007; Sprenger, 2008), you will find that the brain craves the day-to-day structure that comes from the family's established rules, rituals, routines, and responsibilities. Following the same weekday routines or procedures also helps to make the household predictable and stable. When children can depend on life being

Children test their parents to see if the parents are consistent and stable, and they really want their parents to pass the test (Runkel, 2007).

predictable and needs being met, they feel secure and learn that they can trust others and the world in which they live (Nelsen, Erwin, & Duffy, 2007).

For example, if your children are teenagers and know that the rule for curfew is midnight, arguments become unnecessary. If children know that they must make their bed as one of the daily rituals prior to going to school, they learn the responsibility of a well-made bed. By the way, a ritual or repeated behavior does not become a habit in the brains of your children overnight. It takes continuous practice. Remember that for a routine to become a habit, the brain must perform it over and over. The more procedures are practiced, the sooner they become habits (Sprenger, 2007b). Therefore, your children need to make their beds once a day every day for a minimum of 3 weeks if you want them to get in the habit of making their beds each day.

Families who have rituals, or established practices that involve all family members, create a sense of belonging and purpose. Children who are given routine chores to do may have the security and safety of feeling that they belong or are a part of something and can therefore be a comfort to others (Sprenger, 2008).

Many parents today are more concerned about being a friend to their children than being a parent. In fact, if parents derive their own security from the family, their need to be popular with their children may be more important to them than the importance of a long-term investment in the development and growth of their children (Covey, 2004). Children don't need more friends. They have peers who can fulfill that role. What they

> Routines and procedures free the brain's working or short-term memory and its prefrontal cortex to do higher-level thinking (Sprenger, 2008).

do require is a caring, concerned authority figure in their daily lives, one who provides the structure, parameters, discipline, and life lessons so necessary for optimal growth and development. You will have to make decisions your children will not like, but that is all right. Be sure to explain to your children why you are making the decisions that you are and how it is in their best interest. Then stick to your guns! According to Runkel (2007), author of the book *Screamfree Parenting, part of being a grown-up is enduring discomfort now for the sake of a payoff later* (p. 41). Children want and need the rules, rituals, and responsibility their parents provide. Don't feel guilty for providing exactly what they need.

There is a fairly recent term in educational circles known as a *helicopter parent*. These parents can be found across all races, ethnicities, and income levels and are named because of the fact that they *hover over* their children and attempt to take over and take away any personal responsibilities from their children for their own successes or failures. Children whose parents are overprotective or whose parents don't encourage them to overcome anxiety or shyness often become anxious and shy adults (Wingert & Brant, 2005). Even colleges are attempting to deal with this type of parent. For example, the Ithaca College website offers the following advice to parents: *Visit (but not too often); communicate (but not too often); Don't worry (too much); Expect change; Trust them* (Gibbs, 2009, p. 57). Parents who want their children to become self-directed as adults have to face the fact that they cannot do it for their children (Runkel, 2007).

There is even a parent that is more difficult to deal with than the *helicopter parent*. This parent is called the *stealth bomber* because he or she dives in with lists of demands which should be granted on behalf of the child. An example would be the parent who insists that her or his child get the lead role in the school's spring production at all costs. Well, you may ask, what's wrong with that? Wouldn't the child learn valuable life lessons if he or she actually auditioned and earned the role by being the best candidate for it, and, if not selected after auditioning, wouldn't this be a good time for the child to learn how to behave when one does not get everything to which he or she feels entitled? Many adults that I see have not learned this lesson yet themselves, since they were never taught as children!

Just as rules and responsibilities are crucial, so are positive rituals. Visualize when you were little. What were the family rituals or celebrations to which you looked forward? In my family, Sunday dinners were special and all were expected to be present for them; all birthdays were celebrated, even if only with other immediate family members; and the family always took a summer

> The damages of not having any authority with your children are just as horrible as the damages of abusing that authority (Runkel, 2007).

vacation together, even if it meant taking in the local sights and sounds around our city of Atlanta due to a limited budget. Remember, it is not what you do that makes it a ritual. It is that you do it consistently.

Here is probably the most important thing. My children are now creating memories for my grandchildren in the same ways we created memories for them. So many children today have no positive family rituals to remember or to look forward to and for that, I am truly sorry!

HOW CAN I MAKE IT HAPPEN?

○ Parents spend so much time telling their children what not to do, they neglect to tell them the behaviors they expect. Concentrate on telling your children what behaviors you want, not what you don't want. For example, if your child is running in the house, instead of saying *Don't run!* you will want to say *Walk!* It is a subtle but very important difference. It enables the brain to practice the desired behaviors.

○ Explain to your children that it takes contributions from every member of the family to maintain the household. Have your children volunteer or assign them jobs to do around the house. Stress the importance of doing the job well so that the entire family can function effectively. Even preschool children can make their beds, put away their toys, and dress themselves. Remember that when children have chores, it helps to satisfy their need to belong.

○ Establish routines and procedures that can help the family function. If your children are old enough, involve them in conversations about which routines are needed and why. Routines could be centered around getting ready for work and school, preparing meals, cleaning up after meals, completing homework, and getting ready for bed. Once the routines are set, have everyone follow them. Remember that if the routines become habits, children will follow them automatically without much effort. Routines and procedures give the brain automatic responses to ordinary questions that would take up energy and time (Sprenger, 2008).

○ Once the procedures have been established, it is not enough for children to be told what they are; they must be shown. In fact, with the younger children, you might even have to act out or role play what behaviors you expect in certain situations. For example, before going out to dinner at a nice restaurant, you will want to practice the use of the silverware, proper etiquette, conversational voice tone, and so forth.

○ Once the procedures have been taught and practiced, cue your children with a reminder of what the procedures are prior to the event. For example, before taking your 4-year-old to the mall, ask her to tell and show you how she will behave once you get there.

○ If your family has established responsibilities and routines for all, when children do not comply, there should be consequences for noncompliance. Some parents are so busy trying to be their children's friends that they are hesitant to hold them to their commitments. Sit down with your child and discuss the noncompliance, but, as the parent, you owe it to him to expect that he will follow through on his commitments the way he expects you to follow through on yours. See Chapter 10 for additional information regarding consequences.

○ Model for your children the behaviors you expect from them. If you want them to make their beds, yours should be made. If you want them to clean up after themselves, then you should do likewise. If you want them not to smoke, take drugs, or abuse alcohol, then they should never see you engaged in those practices. There is no room for the statement, *Do as I say, not as I do!* Children believe what they actually see you model.

○ Establish rituals, or occasions and activities that children have to look forward to year after year. When I was growing up, every summer, my mother and sisters and I took the train to New York City to visit my aunt and uncle. We were so excited that we could not sleep the night before. The entire family ate big breakfasts and dinners together every Sunday without fail, and Christmas Eve dinner was always extra special. These are just a few of my fondest memories growing up. Make memories with your children that they will never forget. They will pass them on to their offspring.

○ Encourage your children to take on new challenges that will help them grow. For example, my daughter Jessica did not have confidence in her ability to sing until her high school choral director told her how beautiful her voice was. We had told her many times, but she did not believe us. When she was asked to sing a solo in the spring recital, we encouraged her to do so. She gained so much confidence from that experience that she graduated, went on to college, and auditioned for and made the Chamber Chorus at Vanderbilt University. How will your children ever know what they are capable of if they are never allowed and encouraged to try?

ACTION PLAN

> What will I commit to do to ensure that my child(ren) are provided with rituals and learn responsibility?

What am I already doing that I should continue to do?

1. _____
   _____
   _____.

2. _____
   _____
   _____.

3. _____
   _____
   _____.

4. _____
   _____
   _____.

What new habits will I commit to developing?

1. _____
   _____
   _____.

2. _____
   _____
   _____.

3. _____
   _____
   _____.

4. _____
   _____
   _____.

Accentuate the Positive

What we learn with pleasure, we never forget.

—Allen, 2008

WHAT DOES THAT MEAN?

Try this experiment with a member of your family, preferably another adult. Ask this person to put his or her dominant arm straight out to the side of the body. The goal is to not allow you to pull the arm down as you put your hands on the shoulder of that dominant arm and pull. Try the experiment twice. The first time, ask him to think of something that makes him laugh or smile or envision a very positive aspect of his life. As he is recalling positive thoughts, pull down on the shoulder. Then try the same thing a second time, but ask your subject to think of a time when someone made him very, very angry or stressed. As he recalls that unpleasant time, pull down on the shoulder again, just as you did before.

This is what usually happens. When you pull down on the shoulder while the brain is thinking positive thoughts, the arm stays strong and you should be unable to make the arm go down.

When people are happy, the left prefrontal lobe of the brain is activated. This lobe plays an important role in helping the brain pay attention and process new information (Sousa, 2009).

When the person is thinking very angry or stressful thoughts, the same arm usually goes down fairly easily, even though he is trying to keep the arm up.

What does this little experiment prove? When the brain is thinking positively, the brain has confidence. This enables the body to perform at its best. When I teach this concept in my classes, I always use the analogy of an athlete in any sport. How many times have you seen a baseball player get a hit, and that hit gives the player's brain so much confidence that he or she may come back later in the same game and get another hit? A football player who kicks a field goal through the uprights stands a better chance of kicking the next field goal through the uprights. The team that scores first often has the advantage of winning due to the confidence that the initial score provides. Success breeds success!

Conversely, when the brain experiences high states of stress, anger, or fear, the brain is put under threat. Since the purpose of the brain is survival, its job is to defend its owner from the threat, so it sends more blood to the lower, survival levels of the brain and to the arms and legs. Why would you need more blood in the arms and legs? So that you can either fight the threat or run from the threat, whichever will be more effective for your survival. Since the more higher-level thinking parts of the brain do not have as much blood available to them, they do not function as effectively, and a person simply cannot think rationally. Have you ever been so angry with your children that, until you calmed down, you were unable to respond to them in a logical way? Your brain just wouldn't allow it!

Rather than focusing on the negative things that your children are doing, concentrate on the positive, reinforcing those behaviors that are appropriate. One way to positively reinforce appropriate behavior is by using tangibles, things given to your children when they do what you need them to do. Tangibles are often awarded in the real world. For example, when football players perform well, they may earn stickers that are placed on their helmets for all to see. Military men and women have medals and other types of insignia on their uniforms to depict earned ranks and major accomplishments. Actors receive Academy Awards and singers receive Grammy Awards when their performances are noteworthy.

However, tangibles are the least effective type of positive reinforcement. Why? They can kill the brain's internal motivation and, if used too often, can lead your children to ask the question, *If I do that, what do I get?* They will come to expect something for everything they do, and that is not what happens in the real world. People do

> The more parents use bribes or rewards to get children to learn, the less intrinsic motivation and pleasure they get out of it (E. Jensen, 2008).

not get rewarded for everything they do. In fact, rewards don't keep people happy anyway. Many parents think that simply buying *stuff* for their children is enough to show how much they care. I ask them to *Think again!* If you do give a tangible, be sure that your children know exactly why they are receiving it. It is the *why* and not the tangible that is most important.

Another type of positive reinforcement is privileges. Privileges include allowing your children to go to the movies, spend time with friends, or stay out later than usual because they did what they were expected to do. Privileges are probably better than tangibles for the brain, but they are still not the best way to accentuate the positive.

A third—and the most effective—type of positive reinforcement is a social reinforcer. Social reinforcers are positive comments, positive notes, affirmations, celebrations, and other types of positive interaction between you and your child. They work better than tangibles or privileges

> When people do things that make them happy, the brain releases the chemical dopamine, giving them a sense of pleasure and making it more likely that the behavior will be repeated (Sousa, 2009).

since they are used most often in the real world. In fact, I can't remember a single time when my husband has given me a sticker or a Jolly Rancher for cooking a good dinner! However, many times he has told me how much he enjoyed the meal. That comment becomes a social reinforcer. When you do give a positive comment, be sure you are praising your child's effort rather than ability and that the praise is sincere. The emphasis needs to be on the child and what he or she has been able to accomplish so that the appropriate behavior can be repeated.

HOW CAN I MAKE IT HAPPEN?

○ Make sure that your home provides a positive environment for you and your children. Family members should look forward to coming home every day; home should be both physically and psychologically safe, with an absence of threat. Smiles, laughter, close relationships, and a sense of belonging should be inherent in the daily interactions that take place so that even when you have to talk with your children about something that may not be to their liking, your children will know that you have their best interest at heart.

○ Inspire your children to learn naturally for the sake of learning without bribing or coercing them. Since learning is a survival instinct, the brain is naturally motivated to do it (E. Jensen, 2007). In fact, *what we learn with pleasure, we never forget* (Allen, 2008). If you have started with bribes, slowly eliminate them over time. Use the strategies in the second part of this book to help make learning engaging and pleasurable.

○ The saying *Do what I say, not what I do* does not work here. Provide an example for your children of the joy of learning by modeling the behaviors you expect of them. While they are completing homework, complete some written work of your own. While they are reading silently, select your favorite book and read along with them. *A picture is worth a thousand words.*

> When unconditional love and genuine enthusiasm are always present, "Good job!" isn't necessary. When they are absent, "Good job!" won't help (Kohn, 2005).

○ Learn to separate your child's behavior from the way you feel about her personally. While you may not like what she did, she needs to know that her inappropriate act has not changed the unconditional love that you have for her.

○ Rather than waiting for your children to misbehave and then reprimanding them because of it, cue them or remind them of the appropriate behaviors or specific procedures prior to an activity so that they stand a better chance of remembering. For example, when going shopping, remind your children of the behaviors that you expect and, of course, have previously taught them.

○ When you need to address a concern regarding one of your children, sit down and talk with them one on one. Be sure to open the conversation with a positive comment and to close with one. For example, if you have to address a curfew violation with a teenager, you may want to open the dialogue with a comment such as *I really appreciate the way you volunteer to fix dinner on some nights. This makes a huge contribution to this family. Now, let's talk about a concern I have regarding your late arrival home on Friday night.* Once you have both discussed the situation and made a plan on how to address it, show your child some affection and leave him or her comfortable in the knowledge that one poor judgment has not permanently affected your relationship.

○ Whenever possible, provide your children with choice as a positive alternative to rewards. For example, allow them to decide the order in which they will accomplish certain tasks or have them take turns selecting the restaurant where the family will be eating. When children have choice, they experience a measure of control over their environment.

○ Leave positive notes or messages written specifically for your children in strategic places thanking them for something they have done well. For example, place notes on their pillows acknowledging how well they made up their beds or put notes in their book bags complimenting them on improved grades in a specific content area. Leave notes often just telling them that you love them. This will go a long way in strengthening your relationships.

○ To create a positive environment, play music in the home or car with positive, motivating lyrics and an enthusiastic beat. Get the whole family singing along and clapping to the rhythm. Remember that music can change the state of the brain.

○ The brain loves celebration! Celebrate even minor but deserved successes that your children accomplish. Even when they have not done well previously and you see some improvement, let them know that you appreciate their improved efforts. Some sample celebrations include high fives, handshakes, pats on the back, applause, or original cheers when someone in the family does something well! The following poem summarizes the concepts presented in this chapter:

> *"I've got two A's," the small boy cried.*
> *His voice filled with glee.*
> *His father very bluntly asked,*
> *"Why did you not get three?"*

"Mom, I've got the dishes done,"
  The girl called from the door.
Her mother very calmly said,
  "And did you sweep the floor?"

"I've mowed the grass," the tall boy said,
  And put the mower away."
His father asked with a shrug,
  "Did you clean off the clay?"

The children in the house next door
  Seem happy and content.
The same things happened over there,
  But this is how it went.

"I've got two A's," the small boy cried.
  His voice filled with glee.
His father proudly said, "That's great!
  I'm sure glad you live with me."

"Mom, I've got the dishes done,"
  The girl called from the door.
Her mother smiled and softly said,
  "Each day I love you more."

"I've mowed the grass," the tall boy said
  "And put the mower away."
His father answered with much joy,
  "You've made my happy day."

Children need encouragement
  For tasks they're asked to do.
If they're to lead a happy life,
  So much depends on you.

—Author Unknown

ACTION PLAN

> What will I commit to do to ensure that I accentuate
> the positive with my child(ren)?

What am I already doing that I should continue to do?

1. _____
   _____
   _____.

2. _____
   _____
   _____.

3. _____
   _____
   _____.

4. _____
   _____
   _____.

What new habits will I commit to developing?

1. _____
   _____
   _____.

2. _____
   _____
   _____.

3. _____
   _____
   _____.

4. _____
   _____
   _____.

Deemphasize the Negative

When people live with chronic stress, the brain and body not only age prematurely but memory is also inhibited.

—Markowitz & Jensen, 2007

WHAT DOES THAT MEAN?

I have seen parents who are upset with their children, and most times, justifiably so. The children are acting out in a public place and, no doubt, embarrassing their parents. I have seen parents shouting at the top of their lungs or grabbing their children in an effort to discipline them. The next time this happens, remember the saying I gave you earlier: *He who angers you controls you!*

When you yell and scream at your children, your brain goes into survival mode and you are not able to think as logically as you would if you stayed calm. At the same time, your child's brain goes into survival mode as well, and he or she is likely to do or say something that will only make the situation worse. Remember the experiment in the last chapter concerning what happens to the brain when it is put under threat?

> When children are raised in an abusive environment, they learn that in order to get their needs met, they, too, need to be violent or aggressive (E. Jensen, 2010).

The next time that you are very angry with your children, remember this concept, and wait until you calm down before you discipline them. There is a great deal of verbal and physical abuse that happens when parents are so extremely mad that they cannot think. They do or say things then that they would never do or say under normal circumstances and that, at the very least, can cause physical or psychological damage to their children. Even if the parents later apologize, the children will always remember the response and replay the derogatory comment or the physical abuse over and over in their minds. Don't forget that verbal abuse is just as detrimental to your child as is physical abuse! Just because the bruises may not show on the outside does not mean that your child has not been hurt.

When husbands and wives are angry with one another, that is probably not the time to talk it out. Children do not need to witness constant discord between parents anyway. Parents need to wait until they are calmer and then sit down together and discuss the disagreement. If parents talk about the situation while they are angry, they will say something to one another that they will later regret, and even if they apologize, loved ones are still replaying the comment in their brains and it ultimately destroys the relationship.

Another thing that happens when you become upset is that your brain and body begin to produce the stress hormone cortisol and the chemical adrenaline. A little cortisol or adrenaline is not bad for the body. In fact, low to moderate stress is essential to move the brain and body to action. However, high stress is not good for either brain or body. There is a strong correlation between stress and illness, and any current illness is made worse by stress.

> The type of stress that occurs during daily anxiety or fear, major depression, or posttraumatic stress disorder inhibits memory and kills brain cells in the hippocampus (Markowitz & Jensen, 2007).

Large amounts of cortisol or adrenaline deplete the immune system and weaken memory. The body does not respond well under high stress, either. Let's look to athletes as examples. A field goal kicker in football who misses a field goal will often miss the next field goal. A baseball player who makes one error will often make another error. Think of a time when you were under a great deal of stress. You will not forget the experience, but if anyone were trying to talk logically with you or teach you something, you will not be able to remember the content of the talk at that time.

> Negative stress caused by anxiety or threat releases an overabundance of glucocorticoids into a person's system and has the ability to inhibit learning not only in the present but in the future as well (E. Jensen, 2007).

HOW CAN I MAKE IT HAPPEN?

○ When reprimanding or criticizing your child, only 7% of your message comes from the words you say. The other 93% comes from your voice tone, gestures, facial expressions, and other nonverbals, all magnified by the power that comes from being the parent (Kohn, 2005). Watch the 93%, since they communicate more of your message than the words. Even when children don't appear to be listening, they are absorbing negative reactions from you and are more deeply affected by those reactions than they will admit (Kohn, 2005). Remember that you may have more of an impact when your approach is not heavy handed.

○ There are times when you can correct your children's misbehavior in inconspicuous ways. These are called low-profile interventions, and they enable you to stop misbehavior without disrupting the situation. Try these before you try more obtrusive interventions. Examples would include the following:

- Eye contact—Some parents have only to look at their children a certain way and they immediately stop the misbehavior.

- Hand on shoulder—For some children, a hand on the child's shoulder can provide a calming touch when becoming agitated or overactive.

- Proximity—Moving closer to where your children are can serve to lessen their inappropriate behaviors.

- Signals—Parents and children have special signals that enable them to communicate with one another without other people knowing what is happening.

- Ignoring—If children are not hurting themselves and others but are attempting to gain attention, it might be necessary to ignore their actions until the behavior becomes appropriate.

o When you and your children are in an altercation, if they raise their voices, lower yours. Yelling and screaming escalate an already volatile situation and cause the brains of you and your children to move into survival mode. It then becomes difficult to talk rationally and reason the best response to the situation.

o Use *I-messages* when addressing your children's misbehavior as opposed to putting the blame for the misbehavior on your children. *I-messages* take the emphasis off of your children's behavior and tell how the misbehavior is affecting you personally. Examples of I-messages would be, *I cannot allow you to ridicule your sister since we are a family and support one another* or *I was disappointed when I heard from your teacher that you have not been turning in your homework.*

o When you are angry with your children, that is the worst possible time to discipline them. For the reasons that we talked about earlier in this chapter, you are more likely to say or do things that are physically or psychologically harmful or hurtful. Remember that a great deal of child abuse occurs when parents are experiencing high stress or anger.

o When you are very angry with your children, send them to their rooms until you have had a chance to calm down so that the blood can return to the higher-level thinking areas of your brain. Take time and think through how the situation should be handled. Then deal with it calmly and intelligently.

o Refrain from any form of arbitrary punishment with your children. Punishments are disciplinary actions that are decided on the spur of the moment, are usually not consistent from one incident to the next, and are doled out with a great deal of emotion that is based on the state of the parent's brain at the time. Punishment not only makes people mad, erodes the parent–child relationship, distracts children from the issues that are most important, and makes them more self-centered, but it even eventually loses its effectiveness (Kohn, 2005).

o Avoid physical altercations with your children. These would include pushing, shoving, pulling, spanking, or other types of negative physical touches. Some good reasons for avoid-ing spankings include the following: (1) Empathy and logical consequences are more powerful since they teach problem-solv-ing skills; (2) spankings do not teach the behaviors we want our children to emulate; (3) most children would rather be spanked than think about their poor choices; and (4) spankings can have negative effects such as resentment, anger, and revenge (Cline & Fay, 2006).

○ Refrain from using any sarcastic comments that would belittle, demean, or humiliate your children. Frequent criticism is counterproductive because if your children feel that it is impos-sible to please you, then they will stop trying (Kohn, 2005).

○ Talk with your children regarding a case of inappropriate behavior in a calm manner. Be sure you allow your children to share their points of view and listen twice as much as you talk. Allow these four questions to guide your conversation:

- Describe the situation. What happened?

- How did you respond to the situation?

- Was your response appropriate? Why or why not?

- How could you respond differently should this ever happen again?

Since negative emotions are more difficult for children to regulate, when adults talk to them about these emotions children are more likely to learn how to control them (Hirsh-Pasek & Golinkoff, 2003).

○ Decision making is a part of life. One fundamental truth in life is that all of the choices we make have consequences (Runkel, 2007). We are all constantly making decisions that have either positive or negative consequences for our lives. Sports provide a good analogy for this concept. There are established penalties in football or hockey when there are infractions, managers are thrown out of games in baseball when tempers flare, and there are fouls in basketball due to unsportsmanlike conduct. Unlike pun-ishment, consequences are determined ahead of time so that everyone is aware of what they are and people, therefore, make the decision to engage in the behavior or not. Consequences can be administered with less emotion since everyone knows in advance what to expect. For example, when we exceed the speed limit, we know what the consequences can be. You may want to establish consequences for your children's inappropriate behaviors. Establish these ahead of time and make sure your children know what they are.

○ A consequence is defined as something that a child does not want to happen but that is not psychologically or physically harmful. Natural consequences are the best kind to use since they proceed naturally from the infraction and enable the cause and effect of children's actions to *register in their brains* (Cline & Fay, 2006, p. 101). For example, if your children mess something up, they should clean it up. If they hurt someone's feelings, they should apologize and do what is necessary to make it right. If they destroy something that is not theirs, they should earn money and pay to replace it.

○ The removal of a privilege can serve as an appropriate negative consequence. Not to be able to go out on the next Saturday because you chose not to come home on time the last time you were allowed to go out is the removal of a privilege. Not to be allowed to do something that is enjoyed such as playing video games or using the cell phone is also the removal of a privilege.

○ We just talked about consequences. However, don't expect negative consequences alone to change your children's misbehavior. If consequences were the only things needed for behavior change, then prison would not be a revolving door. In fact, the recidivism rate, or the rate at which people return to prison once they have been released, is approximately 67% within the first 3 years after release. While negative consequences are probably a necessary part of life, it is the positive consequences that change behavior over time. Institutions that house some of the most difficult people have negative consequences inherent in the program, but they also attempt to actively engage their patrons and give them a sense of purpose. Recidivism research also relates that prisoners who earn a GED or who acquire a skill are less likely to return once they are released. Find ways to replace your children's negative behaviors with positive ones. Give them a positive purpose. The other chapters in this book enable you to do just that!

ACTION PLAN

> What will I commit to do to ensure that I
> de-emphasize the negative with my child(ren)?

What am I already doing that I should continue to do?

1. _____
   _____
   _____.

2. _____
   _____
   _____.

3. _____
   _____
   _____.

4. _____
   _____
   _____.

What new habits will I commit to developing?

1. _____
   _____
   _____.

2. _____
   _____
   _____.

3. _____
   _____
   _____.

4. _____
   _____
   _____.

Identify Chronic Behavior and Mood Disorders

Even the worst-behaving child is acting that way because he or she is receiving something useful from the misbehavior.

—Kottler, 2002

WHAT DOES THAT MEAN?

I hesitate to write this chapter because behaviors that used to be considered simply different in the past all appear to have some sort of label in the present. In fact, there appears to be a label for everything, and most children's behaviors will not fall into any of these categories. It is important, however, that when you hear about these labels or one is assigned to your child, you understand what the label means.

Before we discuss some labels you are more likely to hear about, let us talk about four major reasons that children cause disruptions in school. I believe that these same reasons are present in homes. First, children may be simply bored. Whether we like it

or not, we live in a world where children are used to being entertained. Without the presence of television, video games, cell
phones, and the computer, many children are at a loss as to how
their time should be spent. There is a saying, *An idle mind is the
devil's workshop.* When children have no purpose and are not kept
productively busy, they may tend to get into trouble. Second, children crave attention and often perceive that they are not getting
the attention they deserve, so they act out to get it. They may even
act in *not so nice* ways. In fact, negative attention is better than no
attention at all. Third, some children seek power or control and
have no idea how to respond when an adult attempts to take from
them what they perceive as their rights. Last, some children feel
inadequate. Due to specific learning disabilities or academic challenges, these students lack confidence and believe that they cannot do what is being asked of them, so they will cover up their
feelings of inadequacy with misbehavior. In school, it is better to
be looked at by your friends as the *class clown.* No one wants to be
seen as the *class dummy*!

Each of these reasons for misbehavior is typical. For example,
poverty, instability, and stress in healthy children can often produce symptoms that mimic ADHD (Morrison, 1995). However,
when carried to extremes, children can manifest the chronic
behavior and mood disorders described in the paragraphs that
follow. To be considered a chronic disorder, the aforementioned
symptoms should be seen not in isolation but as a constellation of
symptoms continuously present over time.

> Students who have constant behavior problems often have very negative feelings about learning, school, and even about themselves (Sousa, 2009).

Before we begin, however,
there is a term you need to
know called *comorbidity.*
Comorbidity refers to the fact
that a single child can have
symptoms from more than one
chronic disorder, so as we dis-
cuss each one, you may recognize symptoms from several disorders in the same child.

The previous chapters in this book have delineated ways parents can lessen the incidence of these chronic behavior and mood
disorders. For example, parents who treat their children with
hostility or are highly critical or abusive are more likely to have
children who are poorly adjusted, have difficulty establishing
relationships with others, and demonstrate behavior problems
(E. Jensen, 2010). However, there are no guarantees. You can do

everything that is appropriate for your children in school and in life and still have children who exhibit signs of the disorders discussed in the paragraphs that follow. Let's examine each disorder and the symptoms that appear to be associated with it.

Attention Deficit Disorder/Attention Deficit Hyperactivity Disorder (ADD/ADHD)

Childhood is a time for activity. However, when children have significantly more difficulty staying still and focusing than their peers, it might be a case of attention deficit hyperactivity disorder (ADHD). Attention deficit does not have to be accompanied by hyperactivity. Children without the hyperactivity may act before they think but are not constantly in motion. ADHD can have a number of causes including atypical brain development, nutritional deficits, fetal exposure to alcohol, drugs, tobacco, or fast-paced and violent images on television. According to statistics, 35% of those with untreated ADHD will drop out of school, 40% to 50% will become involved in antisocial activities, and 70% to 80% will perform below par at work. They will also be at greater risk for automobile accidents as well as depression and personality disorders (Barkley, 2002). Only a licensed professional such as a pediatrician, psychologist, or clinical social worker can diagnose ADHD.

Attention deficit hyperactivity disorder became the most diagnosed school-age disorder in the United States in 2003 (E. Jensen, 2010).

Symptoms of attention deficit hyperactivity disorder include but are not limited to the following:

- quickly beginning but not finishing tasks
- poor time orientation and management
- acting first and thinking later
- poor organizational skills
- inability to delay gratification
- moodiness, defiance, and aggression
- inability to learn from past mistakes or plan ahead
- poor short-term memory

Conduct Disorder

Children with conduct disorder exhibit severe, pathologically driven, antisocial behavior and can be a parent's greatest challenge. These children can exhibit a persistent pattern of violence that impacts the rights of other human beings. Societal factors that appear to contribute to an increase in children with conduct disorder include a decrease in family time, less-structured home life, lack of a positive father figure in the home, and society's increased tolerance for violence. This disorder occurs far more often in males than in females.

> Boys with lower levels of cortisol, or stress hormone, in their brains appear to be unafraid of consequences and retribution and can show symptoms of conduct disorder (E. Jensen, 2010).

Symptoms of conduct disorder include but are not limited to the following:

- disruptive or aggressive behavior patterns
- willfully bullying or hurting others
- no guilt or regard for how others feel
- hurting or killing animals
- lying, stealing, and then not understanding why they are not trusted
- lacking empathy for others
- being physically cruel to others
- blaming others for their problems

Depression

Depression is a chronic, serious, and intense mood disorder that can attack both the mind and the body. While it is thought to be associated with adults, a great many teens also experience it. A person with a major depressive disorder can feel a loss of energy, inability to concentrate, and anxiety and can tend to sleep too much or too little.

> By the age of 19, approximately 28% of young people in the United States will have experienced an episode of major depression (Lewisohn, Rohde, & Seeley, 1998).

Other types of depression include a milder form called *dysthymic disorder* that lasts at least 2 years or *seasonal affective disorder,* in which symptoms occur more often during the winter months. If left untreated, children are more likely to exhibit other adverse behaviors, such as sleep disorders and drug abuse. Rates of depression are equal among males and females before puberty. However, after puberty, women are twice as likely to suffer from depression as men.

Symptoms of depression include but are not limited to the following:

- persistent feelings of sadness or emptiness
- aches and pains that cannot be explained
- loss of friendships
- thoughts of death or suicide
- increased fatigue or lack of energy
- inability to concentrate
- feelings of guilt or worthlessness
- declining academic performance (even though bright, perfection-oriented children can maintain good grades while simultaneously depressed (E. Jensen, 2010.)

Learned Helplessness

When a child fails to avoid an unpleasant stimulus because of previous exposure to painful stimuli that could not be avoided, the condition could be referred to as learned helplessness (E. Jensen, 2010). Since learned helplessness is more a condition than a disorder, it can be more easily treated than some of the others. It is a child's belief that, regardless of how he or she responds to a situation, the outcome will be negative and there is nothing the child can do to change that outcome, so he or she doesn't try. These children appear apathetic, passive, and withdrawn or what some would even refer to as lazy. However, it goes much further than that. Learned helplessness can be caused by any of the following: neglect in the early years of life, an inability to control a traumatic experience,

Research suggests that children could be genetically susceptible to learned helplessness or it could be influenced by environmental factors like anxiety and acute stress (Stein & Stein, 2008).

parents or teachers who have done too much for a child, or a belief that one's failures are due to a defect in one's character since that is what one has been told. When parents overprotect their children from failure, they deprive them of natural consequences and the knowledge that mistakes and struggle are a part of learning. This unconscious enabling can be one of the causes of learned helplessness (E. Jensen, 2010).

Symptoms of learned helplessness include but are not limited to the following:

- unresponsive even when events are shocking
- perceived inability to control circumstances
- lack of assertiveness or hostility when needed
- lack of motivation
- statements such as *Why bother?* or *Who cares?*
- simply going through the motions without feeling
- weight or appetite loss
- inability to socialize

Oppositional Defiant Disorder

Oppositional behaviors in most 18- to 36-month-old children are normal. It is when those behaviors become severe and pervasive that can signal a problem (E. Jensen, 2010). Oppositional defiant disorder (ODD) is characterized by a pattern of hostile, negative, and chronic behavior that lasts for a minimum of 6 months. Children with this disorder tend to show little regard for how others feel and are aggressive and confrontational. It resembles conduct disorder minus the violence and can be caused by a combination of a child's inherent personality; environmental factors such as alcoholic parents or ones who have been in trouble with the law; divorced parents; sexual or physical abuse; environmental toxins; or low levels of serotonin in the brain.

> Oppositional defiant disorder accounts for at least half or more of all mental health referrals and is more common in boys prior to puberty and nearly equal in boys and girls after puberty (E. Jensen, 2010).

Symptoms of oppositional defiant disorder include but are not limited to the following:

- loss of temper

- defying or arguing with adults

- becoming vindictive for no reason

- low self-esteem

- becoming easily annoyed by others

- being resentful or upset

- bothering others on purpose

- use of profanity

Acute Stress Disorders

Low to moderate stress is actually good for us. Having a little adrenaline coursing through our bodies motivates us and enables us to want to do our best. However, an overabundance of stress is called *distress*

Exposure to violence in the family can significantly raise chronic and acute stress levels (Emery & Laumann-Billings, 1998).

and serves as a threat to the brain and body. Distress is a chronic condition that causes cortisol, *the hormone of negative expectations,* to be released (E. Jensen, 2010). Distress impedes memory and creativity, weakens the immune system, diminishes a person's social skills, and can interfere with the process of learning. Causes include prenatal distress, a heart rate greater than 94 beats per minute, a dysfunction in the frontal lobe of the brain, and a chaotic and disruptive home life. *Posttraumatic stress disorder (PSTD),* included in this category, occurs when a person is involved in a life-changing situation such as physical abuse, a loved one's sudden death, or personal illness.

Symptoms of acute stress disorders include but are not limited to the following:

- dreams of and flashbacks to the traumatic event

- a numbness or no response to situations

- hypervigilance, or an increased state or arousal

- difficulty sleeping
- irritability and anxiety
- lost interest in things that were once enjoyed
- increased aggressiveness
- difficulty feeling affection for others

There is a concept in *The 7 Habits of Highly Effective People* that basically says there are two circles in everyone's life: a large circle called the *Circle of Concern* and a smaller circle within that circle called the *Circle of Influence.* The Circle of Concern represents all of the things that we are concerned about but can do nothing about. The Circle of Influence represents those things we are concerned about but that we can also directly influence. (See the diagram below.) People who are under a great deal of stress spend most of their time in the Circle of Concern worrying about all the concerns they can do nothing about. More effective people spend time staying within their Circle of Influence and changing the things they are capable of changing.

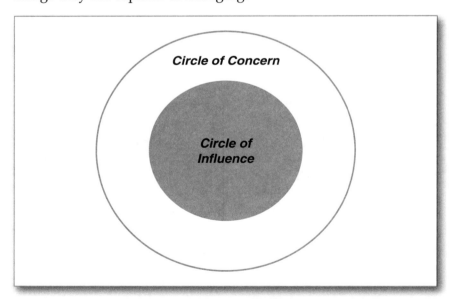

It is the same as the following *Serenity Prayer of Saint Francis of Assisi:*

God, grant me the serenity to accept the things I cannot change,
The courage to change the things I can,
And the wisdom to know the difference.

The reason I am sharing this concept now is that in dealing with children who may have chronic disorders, life can be quite stressful. However, remember to concentrate on those specific things you can do to help these children succeed.

HOW CAN I MAKE IT HAPPEN?

○ I hope you have come to realize that if you fill your child with the concepts contained in Chapters 1 through 10—such as developing a relationship with your child; maintaining a calm, high-challenge but low-stress home environment; giving your children responsibility; and dealing with them in positive rather than negative ways—many of these chronic behavior disorders will never surface in the first place. Don't wait for these behaviors to show up; do everything you can proactively to guard against them.

○ Sometimes, even if you do everything right as a parent, these chronic behavior disorders may still be evident. Maintain a positive attitude regarding your ability to deal with your challenging children and realize that it will take time to see the positive changes you are expecting. Celebrate even small successes toward the ultimate goals.

○ A close relationship with your children should be maintained throughout the process. Try to separate the behavior from the child. You are human, and some things your children do will make you angry. While you are not willing to tolerate those specific behaviors and will work to eradicate them, you should never stop loving your child.

○ Elicit the help of professionals who are more knowledgeable than you in putting together a positive behavior support plan for you and your child. There are people in your children's school system who may be able to assist in this effort. These support people include administrators, classroom teachers, counselors, psychologists, social workers, special education teachers, and others. It is a sign of strength to work within your *Circle of Influence* to get help for yourself and your child.

○ Use the brain-compatible strategies outlined in the second half of this book when assisting your children with homework. These strategies provide the active engagement so necessary for all children, but especially for those who have difficulty learning in more traditional ways. For example, attention spans that seem short can be lengthened when adding the strategy of movement to the learning. The movement anchors thought (Hannaford, 2005). When we found a school where the brain-compatible strategies were used during instruction, our son Chris, who has some symptoms of attention deficit disorder, was successful.

○ If your children are old enough, acquaint them with the 20 strategies and teach them to use selected ones as study skills strategies when they are completing homework or getting ready for tests. For example, if your children can make up a song or rhyme, create an original movement, or draw a graphic organizer to help them retain content, and then they should be encouraged to do so.

○ Some children with chronic disorders need more structure than other children. This structure comes from the routines and procedures that are established early on in the home and discussed in Chapter 8. Make your home schedule predictable so these children have more of a sense of security throughout each day.

○ Remain positive and calm when dealing with children who have chronic behavior disorders. Eliminate the threats, punishments, and otherwise negative responses to the behavior of these children. Their brains may already be producing cortisol, a stress hormone, or adrenaline, which is produced when people are fearful. Adding your accusations and threats just increases the amount of these chemicals in their brains and can make your children more antagonistic, argumentative, or violent than before. They just make the situation and your reaction to it worse.

○ For children who exhibit symptoms of ADD/ADHD, focus on the following: reinforce positive behaviors and rechannel negative ones, avoid threats and distress, provide external reinforcers such as points or extra recognitions, establish routines, use more movement, communicate with them in writing, and teach them how to manage time (E. Jensen, 2010).

○ For children who exhibit symptoms of conduct disorder, focus on the following: provide a positive environment, don't believe their stories without proof, make specific requests, be consistent, give privileges rather than rewards, share your plan with your children, and provide nutritional support (E. Jensen, 2010).

○ For children who exhibit symptoms of depression, focus on the following: incorporate more physical activity; teach goal setting and coping skills; provide proper and balanced nutrition, including a balanced breakfast, complex carbohydrates (cereal, pasta, potatoes), tryptophan (found in milk, turkey, and avocadoes), and protein (lean meats, yogurt, nuts, eggs; E. Jensen, 2010). See Chapter 4 for help with proper nutrition for your child.

○ For children who exhibit symptoms of learned helplessness, focus on the following: engage their brains in positive states, be energetic and enthusiastic, maintain a good relationship, and challenge your children through enriching experiences (E. Jensen, 2010).

○ For children who exhibit symptoms of oppositional defiant disorder, focus on the following: agree upon rewards and consequences in a behavior support plan, respond in a nonconfrontational way, confirm stories before you believe them, and remain consistent (E. Jensen, 2010).

○ For children who exhibit symptoms of stress disorder, focus on the following: be personal and positive and take time to connect with them; use more movement; establish structure and routines; teach stress-reduction techniques such as deep breathing, yoga, singing, visualization, and movement; and encourage goal setting (E. Jensen, 2010).

○ The book *Different Brains, Different Learners: How to Reach the Hard to Reach*, 2nd ed., by Eric Jensen (2010), is an excellent resource for additional strategies in parenting children who have these and other chronic behavior disorders.

ACTION PLAN

What will I commit to do to ensure that I help my child(ren) with chronic behavior disorders, if necessary?

What am I already doing that I should continue to do?

1. _____
   _____
   _____.

2. _____
   _____
   _____.

3. _____
   _____
   _____.

4. _____
   _____
   _____.

What new habits will I commit to developing?

1. _____
   _____
   _____.

2. _____
   _____
   _____.

3. _____
   _____
   _____.

4. _____
   _____
   _____.

Expect the Best and Visualize Success

What you say about your kids is more important than what you say to them.

—Runkel, 2007

WHAT DOES THAT MEAN?

A major study on the effects of expectations on the brain occurred in the 1960s at Harvard University. An experimental psychology teacher by the name of Robert Rosenthal conducted an experiment with his students. He divided them into the experimental group and the control group. The ultimate goal of both groups was to get white mice to run a maze in the shortest amount of time possible. The students in the experimental group were told that their mice had been carefully bred and to expect a great performance out of them. The students in the control group were told nothing. As far as they were concerned, their mice were ordinary lab animals. What do you suppose happened?

You guessed it! The mice in the experimental group ran the maze three to four times faster than the mice in the control group. Actually, there was absolutely no difference between the mice in the two groups. They were all just ordinary lab animals and were randomly assigned to the students. What made the difference? The students in the experimental group used more supportive and motivating behaviors than did those in the control group. They could even be overheard saying, *Go, mouse, go! I know you can do it!* You see, this group had higher expectations for what their mice were capable of achieving.

This experiment was repeated with students in the Los Angeles County School District. Robert Rosenthal teamed with a researcher named Lenore Jacobson to conduct what would become a famous experiment called Pygmalion in the Classroom. Some teachers were told that their class was comprised of students who had been identified as *late bloomers* and to expect improved achievement from these students, even though they had not done as well to this point. Other teachers were given no special information regarding their students. The same thing that happened in the laboratory happened in the classroom. Students in the classrooms where expectations of teachers were higher actually scored higher that year on tests of both achievement and aptitude than did their counterparts in the other classrooms. Research appears to show us that you get what you expect!

Dopamine, a brain chemical or neurotransmitter produced when people are happy, is closely associated with their progress toward a goal such as success in school and in personal relationships (Sousa, 2009).

I am the product of high expectations. Neither my grandmother nor grandfather had a college education. My mother attended college and my father finished college when he was in his 40s. However, education was of primary importance in our household. My sisters and I did not decide whether we would go to college. We were *told* by my parents that we would go to college. That was simply the expectation! Case closed! We also attended schools where the teachers had extremely high expectations of what all students were capable of achieving. In fact, one of my high school classmates has her own television show. I know her as Glenda who sat behind me in English class in high school. You may know her as Judge Hatchett, who has her own court show. Members of my graduating class went on to make major contributions to society in a number of different professions, such as doctors, lawyers, teachers, ministers, and so forth.

My dad died more than 30 years ago, but I believe that he is very proud of the way his children turned out. My oldest sister, Ann, has a doctorate and was one of my French professors at Spelman College in Atlanta. My younger sister Eleanor is the human resources manager for the Atlanta Symphony Orchestra, the Woodruff Arts Center, the High Museum of Art, and the Alliance Theater in Atlanta, and I have enjoyed a wonderful career in the business of educating children, parents, teachers, and administrators. My parents got what they expected!

> The further in school parents believed their adolescents would go, the higher the achievement of their adolescent children, the higher the children's own expectations, and the more time the adolescents spent on homework (Glasgow & Whitney, 2009).

Expect great things of your children and tell them of your high expectations! In addition, visualize their success! Visualization means that you see what you expect in your mind. When you visualize, the same sections of the brain's visual cortex are activated as when the eyes are processing input from the real world (Sousa, 2006). Even athletes visualize themselves performing prior to the actual sporting event. Did you see Lindsey Vonn visualizing her downhill run in the 2010 Winter Olympics prior to skiing it? It must have worked. She won the gold medal in that event! Tennis player Roger Federer also visualizes himself winning every match before the match even begins. Does he win every match? No! But he is definitely one of the best tennis players of all time. My niece Catherine, a fast-pitch softball pitcher, has been taught to visualize herself

> Children can visualize a performance prior to it happening, just like great athletes (i.e., golfers and skiers) and actors do (Caine, Caine, McClintic, & Klimek, 2005).

throwing strikes prior to a game, and she is terrific! Perhaps we will even see her in a future Summer Olympics, if they ever decide to put women's softball back in as an Olympic sport.

Tell your children of your high expectations for their success and then make them believe that those expectations are possible to fulfill. Do not, however, expect that each child will follow the same road to success. Just as your children have different personalities, they also have different learning styles.

HOW CAN I MAKE IT HAPPEN?

○ Let your children know that you expect great things from them and that they are capable of achieving whatever they put their minds to. When people expect positive results, they will expend energy making those results happen. When they expect negative results, they will expend just as much energy on failure (Wong & Wong, 1998). Use terminology with your children that communicates your positive expectations for them. Tell them how much you depend on them and how they are capable of becoming anything they determine they want to be. Become involved in your children's schooling. Your involvement affects their achievement and also influences their educational aspirations and career choices (Hill et al., 2004).

○ Model courtesy in your home and expect it from your children. As society tends to devalue courtesy, we are seeing children who are growing up without it. When I was young, we had to say *No sir* to my father and *Yes ma'am* to my mother. I do not require my children to do the same, but they must say *Yes* and *No*. We do not accept *Yep* and *Nope*. Certain phrases like *Shut up!* or *Talk to the hand!* were never allowed.

○ Remember that there may be as many different personality styles and learning styles as there are children in your home. Therefore, never compare one child with another. Your children should never hear you make these statements: *Why can't you be more like your sister? What was easy for your brother appears difficult for you.*

○ Fifty years of research tend to show that people get what they expect. You have heard of this concept as the self-fulfilling prophecy. For example, if you have a child with some behavioral challenges that upset you, each time this child does anything that is even remotely negative, the response tends to be *I knew you were going to misbehave* since those negative behaviors fulfill your already-established expectations for that child. You even tend not to notice when that child does something right. On the other hand, if you have a child from whom you expect good behavior, then negative behaviors tend to be overlooked in favor of those positive behaviors that reinforce what you already thought about that child. The moral here is to be open to the positive behaviors found even in the most challenging child.

○ I teach a program called *True Colors* that identifies human beings in terms of four personality or temperament types. This concept dates back to the days of Hippocrates, who categorized people as phlegmatic, melancholic, choleric, and sanguine. True Colors correlates this research to the colors gold, blue, green, and orange. Each color has a different strength. Gold children are organized and learn best when things are in sequence. They will keep their rooms neat and tend to be dependable. Blue children are the peacemakers and mediators of the family and value all family members. Green children are always asking *Why?* and use their intellect to problem solve. Orange children are the innovators and risk takers and seek out fun and activity in life. Capitalize on the strengths of each child in your family and use their talents to the family's advantage.

○ The True Colors program also teaches that to be too much of any one color is detrimental. Therefore, help your children to balance their lives so they can honor their strengths while building up their weaknesses. Children who are too gold may become overly organized, bossy, and judgmental and not willing to consider the opinions of others. Children who are too blue are most bothered with any conflict in the family and may become excessive people pleasers. Children who are too green tend to be so intellectual that they lack interpersonal or social skills. Children who are too orange take too many risks and will push the limits of your rules and regulations. Capitalize on each child's strengths and help them make specific plans to strengthen their weaknesses.

○ Help your children set both short- and long-range goals for their lives. With preschoolers, these goals need to be accomplished within a short time span—such as a day or a week. They just can't wait! As children get older, they are more capable of planning long term. Goal setting focuses children's attention on the task in which they are engaged and stimulates the production of endorphins (feel-good brain chemicals) as the brain anticipates achievement of the desired goal (E. Jensen, 2007).

○ Have children visualize, or see themselves, accomplishing the short- and long-range goals they have set for themselves. Ask them where they see themselves in 2 years, 5 years, or 10 years. Visualization is powerful! When the brain sees in the mind, or visualizes, it goes through the same processes that it would go through if the event had actually happened. Once you know their goals, talk with them about the specific action steps it would take for them to accomplish those goals. Put the plan in writing and refer to it periodically.

◌ Allow your children to hear you say positive things not only to them but about them to others as well. Remember to praise their effort at accomplishing a task rather than their ability and give them the confidence to believe they can be successful. Remember that a large percentage of a person's success is due to his or her brain's confidence in his or her ability to succeed. It carries the same weight as innate ability and environment combined. Haven't you seen a sports team that may not have the same high skill level as another team beat that team due to its attitude and belief in its ability to be successful?

◌ The brain likes high challenge but low stress! Encourage your children to try new and different endeavors that may challenge them to expand their mental and physical abilities. After all, how will your children ever know what they are capable of if they never even try? Having children ultimately believe in themselves as capable human beings comes from having them accomplish things that are difficult, not from doing things for them or just telling them they are great (Cline & Fay, 2006). Remember the saying, *What doesn't kill you makes you stronger!*

◌ However, the secret is not letting them lose their confidence in their ability to succeed at something challenging. You want their brains in a state of low to moderate stress, but not high stress. Even if they are not as successful as they want to be, they are much better off for having tried.

◌ The next time you are tempted to lower your expectations for your children, remember the following poem:

I don't cause teachers trouble.

My grades have been okay.

I listen in my classes,

And I'm in school every day.

My teachers say I'm average

My parents think so too.

I wish I didn't know that,

'Cause there's lots I'd like to do.

I'd like to build a rocket.

I've a book that tells you how;

And start a stamp collection;

Well, no use in trying now.

Cause since I found I'm average

I'm just smart enough to see

It means there's nothing special

That I should expect of me.

—Anonymous

ACTION PLAN

> What will I commit to do to expect the best and
> visualize success in my child(ren)?

What am I already doing that I should continue to do?

1. _____
   _____
   _____.

2. _____
   _____
   _____.

3. _____
   _____
   _____.

4. _____
   _____
   _____.

What new habits will I commit to developing?

1. _____
   _____
   _____.

2. _____
   _____
   _____.

3. _____
   _____
   _____.

4. _____
   _____
   _____.

PART TWO

Preparing Children for Success in School

The majority of the brain research began in the 1960s with the work of Dr. Roger Sperry, who was attempting to control the effects of epileptic seizures by severing the corpus callosum, the structure that joins the left and right hemispheres together, in epileptic patients. What he noticed was that these patients appeared to function normally but used one side or the other of their brains depending on the task that was being performed. What we know now is that a left- and right-hemisphere brain theory is too simplistic and that the brain actually uses both hemispheres when acquiring information or performing a task.

The research continued into the 1990s, which were declared The Decade of the Brain, and millions of dollars went into finding cures for such brain illnesses as Alzheimer's and Parkinson's diseases. As a result, much more was learned about this mysterious and miraculously designed organ. For example, remember that the greatest period of growth for brain cells, called dendrites, is from 0 to 4 years of age, but the second major period for brain growth is in early adolescence. This is one reason it is so detrimental for the middle-school brain to be bored. We also know that the brain's frontal lobe houses the reasoning and higher-level thinking functions. This lobe does not fully mature until people are in their 20s, while the feeling area of the brain matures much earlier. This explains why adolescents don't always make good decisions since those decisions are based on emotion and not what is reasonable. The next time your adolescent makes a bad decision, don't get upset. Just calmly say to him or her, *I understand dear, your frontal lobe is not mature yet!*

As a result of my reading, studying, and presenting on brain research, I have come to the conclusion that there are 20 ways to teach so people remember. It really doesn't even matter what theory you examine—Howard Gardner's *Theory of Multiple Intelligences* (1983) or Robert Sternberg's *Theory for Successful Intelligence* (2000)—you will find one or more of these 20 strategies inherent in that theory. I have compiled the list, and it serves as the basis for the five bestsellers I have written for educators known as the *Worksheets* series. Since parents are their children's first and best teachers, you should us these same strategies to help your children understand and remember key concepts. The majority of the strategies are discussed throughout this book and are listed below:

Brain-compatible Strategies

1. Brainstorming and discussion

2. Drawing and artwork

3. Field trips

4. Games

5. Graphic organizers, semantic maps, and word webs

6. Humor

7. Manipulatives, experiments, labs, and models

8. Metaphors, analogies, and similes

9. Mnemonic devices

10. Movement

11. Music, rhythm, rhyme, and rap

12. Project-based and problem-based instruction

13. Reciprocal teaching and cooperative learning

14. Role plays, drama, pantomimes, and charades

15. Storytelling

16. Technology

17. Visualization and guided imagery

18. Visuals

19. Work-study and apprenticeships

20. Writing and journals

These strategies not only increase academic achievement for every single brain but also make teaching and learning engaging and fun! When you examine the list of strategies, you will realize that they are used most often at the lower elementary grades. It is in prekindergarten, kindergarten, first, and second grades where students are more likely to move, sing, draw, and play games. Isn't it ironic that these same four things keep people young as they age: physical movement and exercise, music, drawing or artwork, and playing games. Where did we get the idea that these strategies are not necessary throughout our entire lives? Guess what! They are essential! One of my purposes in life is to get all educators and parents to realize this.

Let me share the rest of the story regarding my son, Chris, since parents all over the world are telling me that their child has similar characteristics to those of my son. When Chris was in the lower grades, he was a straight-A student; as he progressed to middle school, he began to make Cs and Ds. By high school, he was making Ds and Fs. Most teachers at that level were not using the majority of the strategies, and his grades and the grades of other students in his classes suffered. He lost all of his confidence and began to follow students around who were not necessarily ones with whom we wanted him to associate.

We finally pulled him out of the neighborhood high school and his father, Tyrone, found one where teachers were using the strategies. If you know anyone who teaches Reserved Officers Training Corps (ROTC), ask him or her to let you see the curriculum. The strategies are inherent in it. At this school sponsored by the military, called the Youth Challenge Academy, not only did Chris graduate, but he also received the Leadership Award for demonstrating leadership abilities in his group.

Every person has gifts. Let me relate the gifts of my son. Christopher draws beautifully, he can assemble anything with his hands, and he is very technologically proficient. If his middle and high school teachers had used the brain-compatible strategies of drawing, manipulatives, and technology as well as movement, role play, and games, he and other students like him would have been very successful in school. By the way, he is currently pursuing a Bachelor's degree in media arts and animation at the Art Institute of Atlanta and absolutely loves what he is doing. His course of study honors his gifts!

What am I saying to you? When you use the 20 strategies, you uncover more of your children's gifts. You will have ways to address you child's auditory, visual, kinesthetic, and tactile modes of learning. These strategies will not only prepare them for school but will help them to be successful in the real world of work and life as well.

Laugh and Have Fun; It's Good for You and Your Child

What we learn with pleasure, we never forget.

—Allen, 2008

WHAT DOES THAT MEAN?

With what animal should you never play a game? A cheetah (cheater).

What did the number 0 say to the number 8? Nice belt!

Why did the turtle cross the road? To get to the Shell station.

What did the green grape say to the purple grape? Breathe! Breathe!

If these riddles made you chuckle, then I have accomplished my objective. Did you know that laughter, humor, and optimism not only increase the brain's proficiency in learning but also appear to lengthen one's life? Have you noticed the age at which

Laughter is a form of internal jogging since it gets the lungs moving, the blood circulating, and the blood pressure and stress-hormone levels lowering and results in fewer heart attacks for those who have had one previously (Kluger, 2005).

most comedians pass away? George Burns lived until the age of 103, Bob Hope to 100, and Phyllis Diller is still living in her mid-90s. You probably saw Cloris Leachman on *Dancing With the Stars* at the age of 83. Betty White is in the prime of her acting career and she is nearly 90 years old. Of course, there are exceptions. Bernie Mac and John Ritter died at very young ages, but the theory appears to hold true for the majority of comedians.

There appears to be a biological reason for this phenomenon. An increase in oxygen, a decrease in pulse rate, and the production of endorphins (feel-good chemicals) are three positive physiological effects of laughter (Costa, 2008). When you are laughing, the body is also producing T-cells. These T-cells strengthen the immune system and enable the body to fight off disease and illness. Laughter also lowers a child's stress level and increases the number of neurotransmitters that are essential if children are to remain alert and retain content (E. Jensen, 2007). It is recommended that 15 minutes of hearty laughing daily become a part of a healthy lifestyle.

On the other hand, stress appears to be the number-one cause of aging, and there is a positive correlation between stress and illness. Stress not only ages your facial features, making you look older, it also ages your cells and arteries, which means that your body is aging faster than it should be. Just look at how the stress associated with being the president of the United States has aged previous commanders in chief. More recent research is also examining the impact of continued stress on cardiovascular disease. In a study of 11,000 heart attack sufferers from 52 countries, it was found that the year before their heart attacks, patients had been under significantly increased stress and strain from family, finances, and depression when

An emerging body of research is showing that the risk of psychological and social factors such as anxiety, stress, hostility, and depression have almost as great an impact on heart disease as obesity, smoking, and hypertension, traditional medical markers for cardiovascular disease (Underwood, 2005).

compared to 13,000 healthy subjects in the control group (Underwood, 2005).

Laughter also places the brain in a positive state for learning and can defuse many potentially difficult discipline situations. However, please do not confuse humor with sarcasm. Any hurtful remark made to your children that will demean, tease, or deride them not only erodes your relationship with them but also incapacitates their higher-level thinking. Even if your children laugh at the remark, it does not mean the remark has not done its damage. Remember to give your children the respect you expect them to give to you. After all, if your children say something sarcastic to you in return, they may find themselves in a world of trouble.

Here is something that most people do not know. The brain cannot tell the difference between real laughter and fake laughter. If you are not truly tickled, then you can fake the laughter, and the reaction will still be good for your body. This is why there have been more than 1,800 laughing clubs formed in the country of India alone. People are getting together and laughing (fake or real) and finding that their health is being improved.

If people are to be effectively motivated, their needs for survival, belonging and love, freedom, power, and fun must be satisfied (Glasser, 1999). There is even a saying that goes like this: *If you love your job, you will never work a day in your life since it will not be work, it will be play.* This is one of the reasons I will not retire anytime soon. I am simply having too much fun! When you reinforce learning concepts through game playing, not only is the brain having fun, but the learning is also remembered.

HOW CAN I MAKE IT HAPPEN?

○ Give your children something positive to look forward to each day. When they leave for home in the morning, bid them a great day and tell them how much you love them. Even if they do not respond positively, as teenagers often don't, the message still gets across. When they return home, ask them about their day and encourage them to ask the same of you. Really listen to what they have to say. You can learn a great deal just by listening.

○ Some adult personality types are more inherently funny than others. Some adults are better joke tellers than others. Many orange personality types are natural comedians. If you have no confidence in your ability to tell a joke, buy a joke book and pick out appropriate ones to share with your children. The laughter will not only place all brains in a positive state but can add years to your lives. The *Reader's Digest*, which comes out monthly, is a good source of wholesome humor.

○ It is natural for children in the primary grades not to understand the subtleties of a joke since their brains may not yet be developed to that point, but they do enjoy riddles. Older adolescents more easily understand the subtleties of humor, satire, or irony since they have more highly developed language skills than those of younger children (Feinstein, 2009). Buy a book of riddles and allow your children to read one to you each day. Children also enjoy making up their own riddles, so provide time for them to do so. Here are some more that you can share with older children:

- What is black and white and red (read) all over? A newspaper.
- Why did the chicken cross the road? To prove to the opossum that it could be done.
- What do you call a fish that operates on the brain? A neurosturgeon.
- Why did the scientist not have a doorbell on his front door? He wanted to win the no bell (Nobel) prize.
- Why did the parrot put on a raincoat in the storm? He wanted to be polyunsaturated.

○ Select a funny movie that would be appropriate for your children and plan a time to sit and view it together. Laugh out loud! University of Maryland School of Medicine found that 15 minutes of watching a humorous movie not only increased blood flow but also relaxed people's peripheral arteries for as long as 45 minutes afterward (Underwood, 2005).

○ If you have older children, help to develop their higher-level thinking skills by introducing them to editorial cartoons. These can be found in the daily newspaper and magazines and are often difficult to interpret since the meanings can be subtle and depend on a reader's background of experiences. Sit down with your older children and discuss the meanings behind some of these cartoons.

What can be one of the most stressful times of the day can be turned into one of the most productive times when parents and children sit down together and actually enjoy completing assigned schoolwork. The use of games is a good strategy for reviewing content that your children need to remember. Games not only raise the level of natural feel-good chemicals in the brain but also, in proper amounts, can increase cognition and working memory (E. Jensen, 2007). In addition, games help children pay attention and focus and are motivating and a great deal of fun (Algozzine, Campbell, & Wang, 2009a).

The next few activities will provide you with ways to review content through the use of games.

○ Buy a Nerf ball or any other soft ball and as you review content, toss the ball to your child. The child must catch the ball and then give you the answer to the question you asked. For example, this is a great way to review multiplication facts. Ask you child, *What is 6 × 8?* Then toss the ball. Your child should catch the ball and then answer *48.*

○ Find a generic game board, such as the one in the game Candy Land, with a starting and finishing point. Make game cards according to the concepts that need to be reviewed. For example, if you are working on vocabulary with your child, put one vocabulary word on each index card and turn them face down in the middle of the table. Then play against your child. Take turns rolling a number generator, or die, and then moving a marker along the game board. However, in order to move, you or your child must identify the same number of words as the number rolled. For example, if your child rolls a six and can name only two words, then he or she can only move two spaces. The same words may be reviewed over and over since repetition is good for the brain. The first player to get to the end of the game board wins, but more important, your child has spent time having fun while reviewing vocabulary. This game can be used in many different ways such as reviewing addition, subtraction, multiplication, or division facts or to recall the definitions of words. Simply change what is written on the index cards.

○ Have your children play Concentration by making 15 matched pairs of vocabulary words and their definitions. Have them write each word on one index card and the accompanying definition on another card. Have them spread the word and definition cards out on a table face down in random order. Take turns with your child trying to match a word to its definition by turning up any two cards on the table. If the cards match, the player keeps the cards and gets another turn. If the cards do not match, they are turned back over in their original place on the table and the turn proceeds to the other player. The player that has the most matches at the end of the game wins. Adapt this game to any other content area. Your child can match a math problem to its answer or synonyms or antonyms to one another.

○ Play Bingo with your children by providing them with a 4 × 4 Bingo sheet containing 16 blank spaces. Select 16 vocabulary words that need to be reviewed. Have your child write the words to be reviewed randomly in any space on the card. You do the same. Have them write the definition of each word on separate index cards, mix them up, and put them in a box or can. Take turns selecting a definition card from the box and reading the definition aloud. As the definition is read, the accompanying word is covered with a marker. Markers can be made from dried beans or peas or even colored construction paper, which enables you to reuse the card. The first player to cover four words in a row, either horizontally, vertically, or diagonally, shouts out *Bingo!* and wins the game. However, to win, your child must give the definition of each word that comprises the Bingo. If your child cannot supply the definition, play continues until you win or your child wins in a different way.

BINGO

○ Show your children how to create Hink Pinks. A Hink Pink is a two-word rhyme where both words are one syllable. For example, an angry father would be a *mad dad*. An overweight feline would be a *fat cat*. If Hink Pinks are too easy for your children, try a Hinky Pinky. A Hinky Pinky is a two-word rhyme where both words are two syllables. For example, military meat sauce would be *navy gravy*. Suppose those are also too easy. Challenge your children with a Hinkety Pinkety. A Hinkety Pinkety is a two-word rhyme where both words are three syllables. For example, the White House would be *the president's residence*. You can even create a clue for two four-syllable words that rhyme. I am not sure what you call them, but they are a lot of fun to create. Here is one. An average administrative assistant is called *an ordinary secretary*.

○ Consult my series Engage the Brain Games at the Corwin website at www.corwin.com for additional game ideas that can be used with your children. Books for grade levels kindergarten through Grade 5 have activities in the content areas of language arts, math, science, social studies, music, and physical education all in one grade-level book. There is a separate book in each of the following four content areas: language arts, mathematics, science, and social studies for Grades 6 through 8 (Tate, 2008).

ACTION PLAN

> What will I commit to do to ensure that my child(ren)
> and I see the humor and optimism in life?

What am I already doing that I should continue to do?

1. _____
_____
_____.

2. _____
_____
_____.

3. _____
_____
_____.

4. _____
_____
_____.

What new habits will I commit to developing?

1. _____
_____
_____.

2. _____
_____
_____.

3. _____
_____
_____.

4. _____
_____
_____.

BINGO

Strengthen Your Child's Auditory Mode of Learning

Tell me, I forget!

—Old Chinese Proverb

WHAT DOES THAT MEAN?

Have you ever said this to your children: *How many times do I have to tell you…?* The Chinese knew thousands of years ago that to tell someone something is probably the least effective way of getting them to remember it. However, when the brain is engaged during the conversation, memory improves. Why is this the case? When people open their mouths to speak, oxygen is sent to the brain. The brain craves oxygen. In fact, if brains are deprived of oxygen for approximately 3 to 6 minutes, people literally become brain-dead. I have been in some classrooms where students were breathing but you couldn't tell! When the brain is not getting enough oxygen, the mouth opens and a yawn occurs. Notice that you seldom yawn when you are active; you are more likely to yawn when you are sleepy, bored, or tired. In the 2010 Winter

Olympics, speed skater Apolo Anton Ono, the most decorated Winter Olympian of all time, purposefully yawned before each race to send more oxygen to his brain cells.

Oxygen can also improve attention and memory for your children. What we talk about, we stand a better chance of remembering. In fact, there are three brain-compatible strategies on the list of 20 that not only send oxygen to the brain but also increase alertness and attention and improve the likelihood that what your children hear will be remembered. They are storytelling, reciprocal teaching, and discussion.

Storytelling

Try telling your children the following story to help them learn the continents. It will take less than 1 minute.

> There once was a man named **North**. His last name was **America**. He fell in love with a beautiful woman named **South**. They got married and she took his name so she became **South America**. They honeymooned in **Europe**. This couple was blessed to have four daughters whose names all began with the letter A. Their names were **Africa**, **Antarctica**, **Asia** and **Australia**.
>
> The End (Tate, 2010, p. 107)

By the time you have told that story to your children at least three or more times and they have told it to you three or more times, they should be able to recall the continents. Why were they so easy to remember? Because all seven continents were connected together in a story, and the brain remembers more easily when ideas are connected together. Storytelling also improves a child's ability to listen and reason since it uses the auditory modality with the frontal lobes of the brain to follow the plot (Storm, 1999).

The concrete images in stories activate emotions and sense of meaning and provide context and cues for new information (Markowitz & Jensen, 2007).

To prove that the brain thinks in connections, try this activity with a family member. Tell the person that you are going to ask him or her a series of questions and you expect quick answers. Then hold up a piece of white paper and ask, *What color is this paper?* (The response will be *white*.) Then quickly ask, *What do cows drink?* (The response should be *milk*, even though cows drink water.) Why? The person's brain connected the word *white*, which is in short-term memory, to the words *cow* and *drink* in the second question.

If you don't believe in the power of story, you soon will. In fact, children's natural fascination with and sense of story never ends. It continues throughout their lives (Caine, Caine, McClintic, & Klimek, 2005). The next time you are listening to a speaker, watch what happens when the speaker begins to tell a story. Everyone in the adult audience is paying rapt attention. Stories have beginnings, middles, and endings, and the brain can follow a story. If the story tends to be emotional, it can have an even more powerful effect on the brain. When you make up and tell a story to your children or when you allow them to make up their own stories, retention of information occurs.

Reciprocal Teaching

Another way to help your children remember content is to have them reteach you what you are teaching them. By the time children are 6, they will love to use their inner speech to teach others, especially adults, and guide those adults through a step-by-step process (Sprenger, 2008). Research has shown that in schools, even average and low achievers, with or without learning disabilities, exhibited increased achievement when provided with opportunities to teach the entire class, small groups, or partners (Tileston, 2004). Reciprocal teaching is also the reason college and university students have gotten together for generations to form study groups outside of class, realizing that if they talked about the course content and retaught it to their peers, they would stand a better chance of understanding and recalling it.

> People remember 95% of what they teach to someone else (Glasser, 1990).

Reciprocal teaching worked for a teacher in one of my workshops. She related this story to me. Her husband was interviewing for a prestigious position at a major corporation. As a part of the application process, he had to pass a test that would necessitate remembering a great deal of information. After taking one of my classes in which we discussed the power of reciprocal teaching, the teacher went home and told her husband to teach everything he needed to know for his test to her, realizing that if he could teach it to her, he had a better chance of remembering it on the day of the test. He remembered! She e-mailed me

> Share what you know and feel memories grow (Sprenger, 2007a).

following the test and told me that he made one of the highest test scores ever on the exam. This experience further convinced her of the power of reciprocal teaching for improving understanding and memory.

Discussion

The brain remembers 90% to 95% of what it discusses with someone else. Therefore, when your children have a problem or when you need to get information across to them, it is beneficial to take turns brainstorming solutions or sharing ideas. When helping with homework, take the time to engage your children in discussions

> Children understand a topic better when they talk about it since their brains process the information not only mentally but also verbally (Allen, 2008).

regarding the content to be remembered. Begin by asking questions to which the answers are stated directly in the text. Then proceed to more challenging questions in which your children have to *read between the lines* or use details in a story to figure out what the answers might be. In the following section of this chapter, you will find some questions that can be used to guide a discussion of content with your children. When you are helping with homework, engaging them in a discussion will greatly improve their ability to recall later the content discussed.

HOW CAN I MAKE IT HAPPEN?

○ Make up a game that can help your preschool and primary-grade children see the difference between the sounds in words. Call out two words and ask them to tell you which words rhyme and which do not rhyme. For example, *dog-log, cat-fat, face-make, man-can, sit-pig*. You might want to see if they can recognize whether words have the same beginning sounds, such as *big-bat, top-map, fish-face, hat-him*. Once they are successful with beginning sounds, try ending sounds, or even vowel sounds. Continue the game using words around the home to see if your children can discriminate the different sounds that they hear. This skill is very important for a beginning reader.

○ When giving directions, remember that the adult brain can only hold between five and nine things at one time, or an average of seven. It is helpful that so much in the real world comes in series of seven—days in the week, colors in the rainbow, notes on the scale, phone numbers, continents, dwarfs, and so forth. Children appear to be able to hold a lot less than seven. Up to age 3, expect them to hold one direction, such as *Go get your coat*. Four- and 5-year-olds can hold two, such as *Put on your shoes and go get your coat*. Six- and 7-year-olds can hold three. Eight- and 9-year-olds can hold four, and so forth. Remember not to expect the brains of your children to hold too many different directions at one time.

○ Remember that the brain needs to hear information at least three times before it begins to stick. If you don't believe that is true, consider what happens when you are not at home and someone leaves a message on your answering machine. Do you often have to play the message back more than once to get the whole message, especially if there is a phone number to be remembered? It is even more important with children that content be repeated. Therefore, when working with them, review what they need to know more than once.

○ When helping your children remember content, take the content and connect it together in a story. Tell the story to your children several times and have them tell it back to you several times. Watch their memories improve. When your children are taking a test at school, they will remember your story and remember the content!

○ When reading aloud to your children, stop periodically and have them retell you a part of the story just read. Not only does the talking get more oxygen to your children's brains, but it also engages them and assists them in recalling the story.

○ Students often remember stories better when those stories are original creations (Allen, 2008). Have your older children create their own stories connecting concepts that they want to remember. When they remember the story, they remember the concepts.

○ The next time you take your child to the library or a bookstore, look for storybooks that teach concepts your child may be learning in school. Take the books home and read them aloud to your children or allow them to read the books themselves. The fact that the concept is presented in a story makes the concept more meaningful. A list of children's book titles, their authors, and the concepts that can be used to teach are as follows:

Sample Children's Books

Title	Author	Concepts
The Important Book	Margaret Wise Brown	Main Idea and Details
The Day Jimmy's Boa Ate the Wash	Trinka Hayes Noble	Cause and Effect
Thomas' Snowsuit	Robert Munsch	Sequence of Events
The Pain and the Great One	Judy Blume	Point of View
Encounter	Jane Yolen	Point of View
My Brother's Flying Machine	Jane Yolen	Point of View
The King Who Rained	Fred Gwynne	Figurative Language
Amelia Bedelia Series	Judy Blume	Figurative Language
The Parts of Speech Series	Brian Cleary	Parts of Speech
The Parts of Speech Series	Ruth Heller	Parts of Speech
The Doorbell Rang	Pat Hutchins	Concept of Division
Counting on Frank	Rod Clement	Real-World Math
Math Curse	John Scieska	Real-World Math
Science Alphabet Books Series	Jerry Pallotta	Science Concepts

   ○ Since the brain learns what it is able to teach to others, stop periodically when helping with homework and have your children teach to you what they are trying to understand or remember. If they can teach the concept correctly, they understand it. According to David Sousa (2006), author of *How the Brain Learns*, the teacher should become the learner and the learner should be the teacher at some point in every lesson.

   ○ Take turns reading a story aloud to your children. Stop periodically and have your children explain to you what was just read. You may want to ask some of the questions listed next to guide their explanation.

Possible Guiding Questions

- What happened in the story?
- What does this word mean?
- Who are the main characters?
- What is the story mostly about?
- Predict what would happen if…
- What happened first, next, last?
- Tell how, when, where, or why.
- Which is a fact? Which is opinion?
- What is the relationship between…?
- What conclusion can we reach?
- How can we solve the problem?
- What else might have happened?
- What might be another ending?

Use the question stems listed above to engage your children in a discussion related to academic work or even personal situations. Remember that there is more than one answer to most questions and allow your children to discuss a variety of ideas. Using questions is a great way to help children understand the ideas and skills they are learning while remembering a great deal of information at the same time (Caine et al. 2009).

ACTION PLAN

What will I commit to do to strengthen my
child(ren)'s auditory mode of learning?

What am I already doing that I should continue to do?

1. _____
_____
_____.

2. _____
_____
_____.

3. _____
_____
_____.

4. _____
_____
_____.

What new habits will I commit to developing?

1. _____
_____
_____.

2. _____
_____
_____.

3. _____
_____
_____.

4. _____
_____
_____.

Strengthen Your Child's Visual Mode of Learning

Tell me, I forget!

Show me, I remember!

—Old Chinese Proverb

WHAT DOES THAT MEAN?

The saying *A picture is worth a thousand words* is more accurate than you realize. It is the reason your children will pay more attention to what you actually do than to what you say. How can you tell if you are more of a visual learner? When your children bring notes home from school and want to read them aloud to you, if you ask them politely to allow you to read it yourself so that you can comprehend what the teacher is saying, you are probably a visual learner.

Three brain-compatible strategies take full advantage of the brain's ability to take in information visually and should be used with all children. They are visuals, visualization, and graphic organizers.

Visuals

When working with students, images and pictures should be provided since the eyes can take in 30 million pieces of information per second (E. Jensen, 2007).

I read in a recent article that the visual cortex in the brains of many children today is actually physically thicker than the visual cortex in my brain when I was their age. Why? Just look around. Children today are watching countless hours of television, challenging their level of expertise on multiple-skill-level video games, and using the computer for a variety of time-consuming tasks. Is it any wonder that the visual modality is a preference for many of today's children?

Visual learners take in the world through words and through pictures (Sprenger, 2007a). What are some instances in which visuals are used in the real world to facilitate memory? Sports teams watch footage following a game to ascertain the level of play and analyze performances. If you have flown in an airplane recently, you know that it is not enough for flight attendants to tell you what to do with your seat belt. They must show you! You must either watch a flight attendant pointing out the specifics, such as the use of the seat belt or the location of the exits or, on the larger flights, you are viewing a video on a television screen that does the same thing. Speakers who use visuals to accompany their speeches tend to have more memorable presentations.

When working with your children, any time you can provide an accompanying visual for them, please do so. It will help the idea stick to their brains!

Visualization

Visuals are things you can see. By contrast, visualization means seeing within your mind, and it can be so effective that it appears

Everything happens twice—once in the mind and once in reality (Covey, 2004).

when visualizing, the brain goes through the same processes it would if it were actually experiencing the event. Imagery or visualization changes the chemistry of the body since it gives humans more mind/body control (Markowitz & Jensen, 2007).

This is why athletes consistently use this strategy as described in an earlier chapter. The Blue Angels Fighter Squadron pilots sit in a room prior to performing their routine. While the pilot in the lead plane tells the other pilots what to do, all pilots visualize the performance while still in the room and then get in their planes and execute what they have visualized. I understand that at St. Jude's Children's Research Hospital, there is a visualization wall. Patients and their parents look at the wall and visualize the children healthy. I do not think that wall would be there if there was not something to the power of visualization.

Some people have difficulty visualizing or seeing in their minds. When children spend many hours looking at the explicit, vibrant visuals that video games and computers exhibit, they have no need to use their imaginations to picture what is happening. It is all right there before them in living color. However, it is thought that it is more effective for young children to be producing their own visual images than having the computer or video game provide those images for them (Healey, 2004). A vivid imagination that is also humorous, fun, or absurd creates images that stay with the brain (Markowitz & Jensen, 2007).

Graphic Organizers

Mind, concept, or semantic maps and word webs can all be categorized under the heading graphic organizers. Graphic organizers depict major ideas and are useful to both the left and right hemispheres of the brain. Those children who are strong in the left hemisphere can easily see the separate details of a concept written in words, while those strong in the right hemisphere can view the pictures or see the major concepts as a whole.

> Graphic organizers gain the attention of children and also improve comprehension, meaning, and retention (Sousa, 2007).

Graphic organizers not only *make thinking and learning visible* (Fogarty, 2009, p. 112), but they also enable children to organize data into chunks or segments that they can comprehend and manage (Gregory & Parry, 2006).

The following sample graphic organizer illustrates the two hemispheres of the brain and delineates the function of each hemisphere. Notice that the graphic organizer depicts two chunks of the brain. Although people have preferences as to which hemisphere appears to work better for them, the research is showing us that both hemispheres work together in all brains and actually talk to one another over a group of nerve fibers known as the corpus callosum.

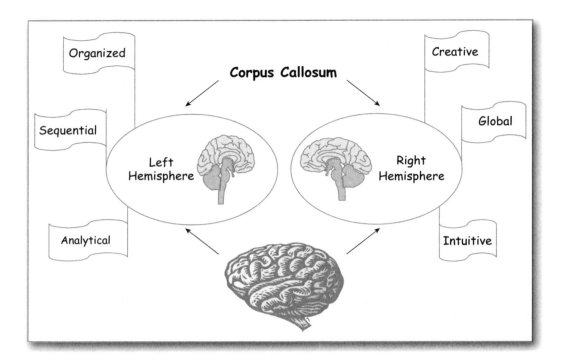

HOW CAN I MAKE IT HAPPEN?

○ Since your children will believe what they see you do more than they will believe what they hear you say, be certain you are modeling the behaviors you expect from your children. You are providing a visual for them. If you want their respect, they should see you respecting yourself and others. If you want to teach them to be patient, they should observe you handling situations with calm. Remember that *actions speak louder than words!*

○ For preschoolers, labeling certain objects in the house, such as bed, chair, table, may provide visuals that, in time, will help your children associate the letters in the spelling of the words with the objects themselves.

○ When helping your child with homework, *a picture is worth a thousand words.* Provide a visual for what you are trying to teach. If you are reviewing an unfamiliar vocabulary word, particularly a noun, showing your children a picture of the word or the object itself may help.

○ When working with the spelling of words, write the letters in the word or have your children write the letters in the word on paper. For an added treat, write the word with different colored markers or crayons.

○ When reading science or social studies textbooks with your children, you may find that it may be difficult for them to understand what is being read. Before you read a chapter, have your children turn the pages and look at the visuals provided, including any chapter titles and subtitles, bold headings, maps, charts, graphs, and other pictures. Have them make predictions as to what the chapter will include. Then have them read sections to see if their predictions are accurate.

○ Read aloud to your children, no matter their ages. As you read, have them visualize the action in the story. Ask them to involve all of the senses (sight, hearing, touch, taste, and smell) in imagining the plot in the story. You might even want your listeners to stop periodically during the story and tell you what they are experiencing so you know whether what they are visualizing is accurate.

○ Write a word on paper and have your children study it for a few seconds. Then take the word away and have them visualize the word or see it in their minds. Ask them to pronounce or spell the word, depending on what you need your children to do. Then show them the word again and allow them to see if their visualization was correct.

○ When helping your children remember the definition of a word, create a crazy visualization to help them associate the word with its definition. The sillier the visualization, the easier it will be for them to remember. For example, when my daughter Jennifer was studying Shakespeare's *Romeo and Juliet*, we were reviewing the vocabulary and she could not remember the definition of the word *scullery*. I used the following visualization. I told her to visualize a skull lying in the middle of a large black and white tile kitchen floor. To this day she still remembers that a scullery room is one off the kitchen in a house.

○ Since the brain thinks in chunks or connections, as you and your children study vocabulary, have them use the following word web to brainstorm additional words that mean the same thing as the word in the middle box. You might want to have your children keep their word webs in a notebook and add to them throughout the year. For example, if the word *happy* is in the middle box, the words in the circles could include the following: *glad, joyous, ecstatic, enthused, jubilant,* and *exhilarated.* (See reproducible page at end of chapter.)

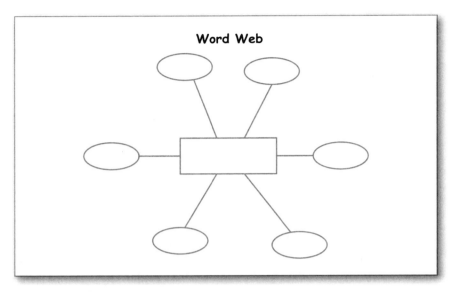

○ A story map or frame is a graphic organizer that can help your children understand the important elements of the plot of a story or novel. As you read a story, use the following story map to help them understand the most important parts. (See reproducible page at end of chapter.)

Story Map

Title: _____

Setting:

Characters: _____   _____
_____   _____
_____   _____

Problem:

Event 1 _____
Event 2 _____
Event 3 _____
Event 4 _____

Solution:

○ Use the following graphic organizer to help your children understand that the details of a story can add up to the main idea. Then, as you read a story, help them to select specific details that can add up to the main idea. (See reproducible page at end of chapter.)

Main Idea/Details

Details

Main Idea

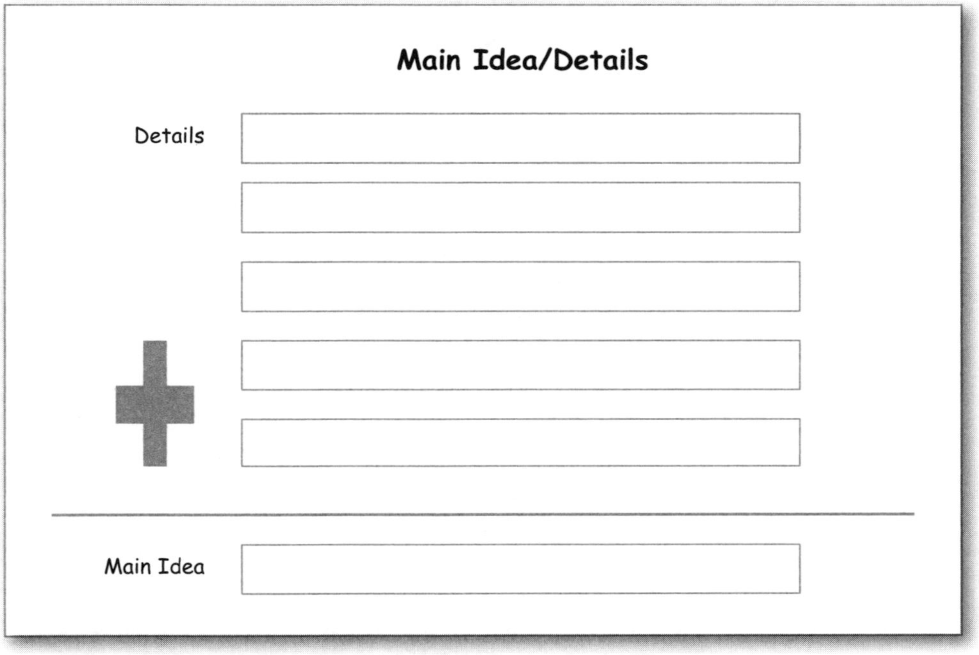

○ Have your children identify cause-and-effect relationships by using the following graphic organizer. Help them to understand that every action results in a certain effect. (See reproducible page at end of chapter.)

Cause/Effect

So

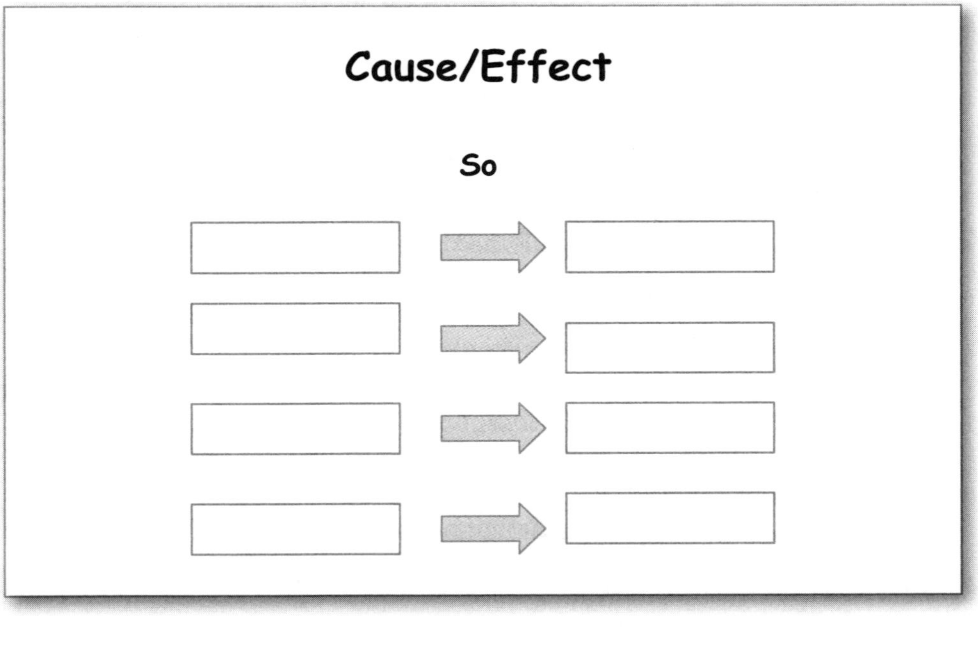

○ Have your children complete the following graphic organizer to identify the order in which things happen and how one event can lead to another. (See reproducible page at end of chapter.)

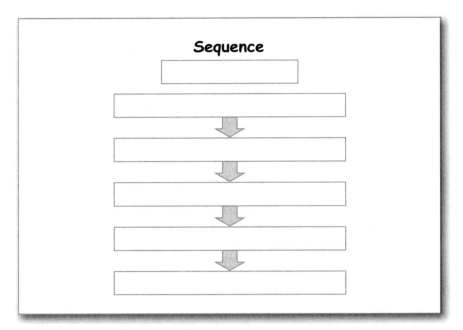

○ Have students compare and contrast two or more characters or events in narrative or content-area texts by using the following Venn diagram. (See reproducible page at end of chapter.)

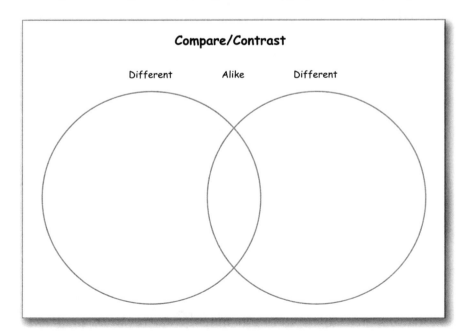

○ Create an original graphic organizer or mind map by using the following format. A mind map is similar to an outline, but it enables your children to see the whole picture at one time. Put the topic in the middle of the mind map surrounded by major ideas springing from the topic. Then other details can be added to each major idea. When your children study for tests, have them review their mind maps and the concepts will be better remembered. (See reproducible page at end of chapter.)

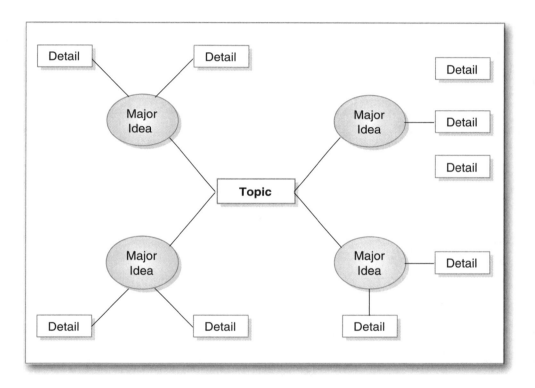

○ Refer to my series *Engage the Brain: Graphic Organizers and Other Visual Strategies* to find additional graphic organizers in the content areas of language arts, math, science, and social studies. For Grades K through 5 all of the content areas are contained in the same book. Grades 6 through 8 have separate books for each of the four content areas of language arts, math, science, and social studies. Consult the Corwin Press website at www.corwin.com for information.

ACTION PLAN

What will I commit to do to strengthen my child(ren)'s visual mode of learning?

What am I already doing that I should continue to do?

1. _____
   _____
   _____.

2. _____
   _____
   _____.

3. _____
   _____
   _____.

4. _____
   _____
   _____.

What new habits will I commit to developing?

1. _____
   _____
   _____.

2. _____
   _____
   _____.

3. _____
   _____
   _____.

4. _____
   _____
   _____.

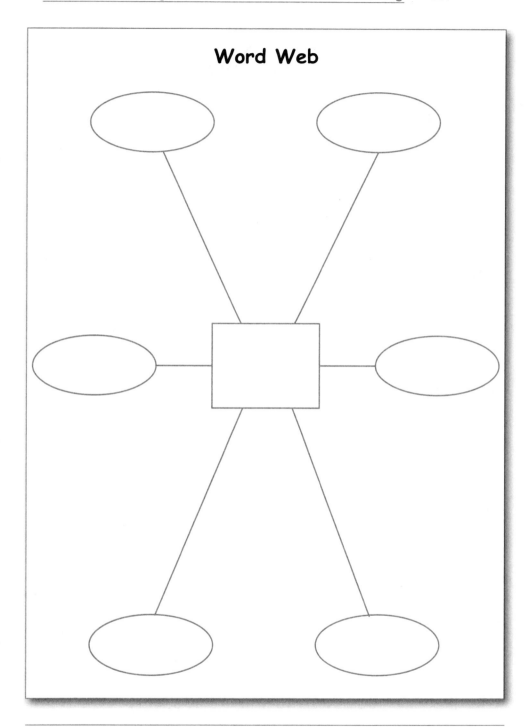

Word Web

Copyright © 2011 by Corwin. All rights reserved. Reprinted from *Preparing Children for Success in School and Life: 20 Ways to Enhance Your Child's Brain Power* by Marcia L. Tate. Thousand Oaks, CA: Corwin, www.corwin.com. Reproduction authorized only for the local school site or nonprofit organization that has purchased this book.

Story Map

Title: _____

Setting:

Characters: _____ _____

_____ _____

_____ _____

Problem:

Event 1 _____

Event 2 _____

Event 3 _____

Event 4 _____

Solution:

Copyright © 2011 by Corwin. All rights reserved. Reprinted from *Preparing Children for Success in School and Life: 20 Ways to Enhance Your Child's Brain Power* by Marcia L. Tate. Thousand Oaks, CA: Corwin, www.corwin.com. Reproduction authorized only for the local school site or non-profit organization that has purchased this book.

Main Idea/Details

Details

Main Idea

Copyright © 2011 by Corwin. All rights reserved. Reprinted from *Preparing Children for Success in School and Life: 20 Ways to Enhance Your Child's Brain Power* by Marcia L. Tate. Thousand Oaks, CA: Corwin, www.corwin.com. Reproduction authorized only for the local school site or nonprofit organization that has purchased this book.

Cause/Effect

So

Copyright © 2011 by Corwin. All rights reserved. Reprinted from *Preparing Children for Success in School and Life: 20 Ways to Enhance Your Child's Brain Power* by Marcia L. Tate. Thousand Oaks, CA: Corwin, www.corwin.com. Reproduction authorized only for the local school site or nonprofit organization that has purchased this book.

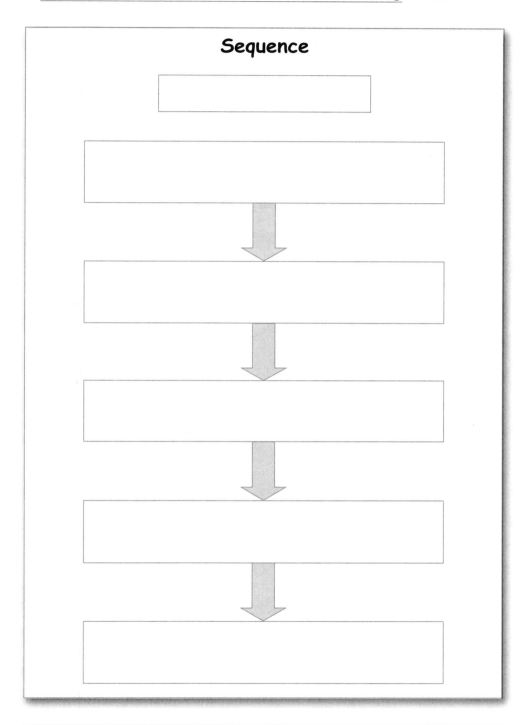

Sequence

Copyright © 2011 by Corwin. All rights reserved. Reprinted from *Preparing Children for Success in School and Life: 20 Ways to Enhance Your Child's Brain Power* by Marcia L. Tate. Thousand Oaks, CA: Corwin, www.corwin.com. Reproduction authorized only for the local school site or nonprofit organization that has purchased this book.

Compare/Contrast

Different   Alike   Different

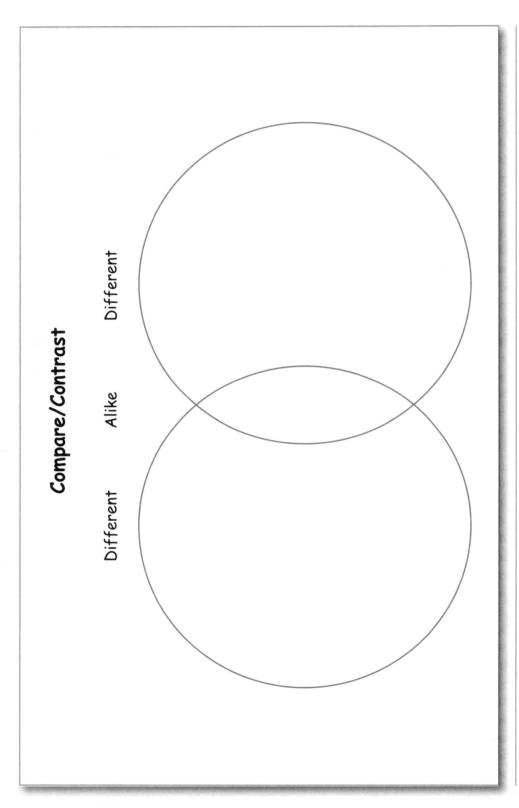

Copyright © 2011 by Corwin. All rights reserved. Reprinted from *Preparing Children for Success in School and Life: 20 Ways to Enhance Your Child's Brain Power* by Marcia L. Tate. Thousand Oaks, CA: Corwin, www.corwin.com. Reproduction authorized only for the local school site or nonprofit organization that has purchased this book.

Main Idea and Details

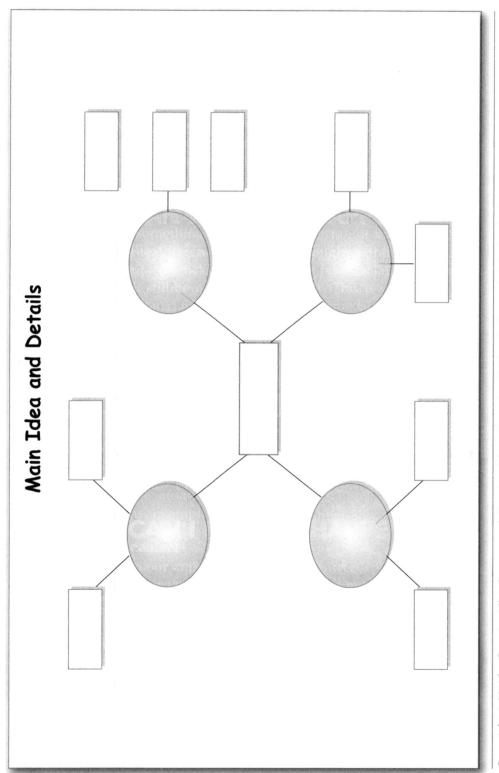

Copyright © 2011 by Corwin. All rights reserved. Reprinted from *Preparing Children for Success in School and Life: 20 Ways to Enhance Your Child's Brain Power* by Marcia L. Tate. Thousand Oaks, CA: Corwin, www.corwin.com. Reproduction authorized only for the local school site or nonprofit organization that has purchased this book.

137

Strengthen Your Child's Kinesthetic Mode of Learning

Tell me, I forget!

Show me, I remember!

Involve me, I understand!

—Old Chinese Proverb

WHAT DOES THAT MEAN?

I have very good news! Mostly anything you learned while you were physically involved or moving is more likely to end up in long-term memory. Even the Chinese knew this fact thousands of years ago; thus, the proverb above. This memory system in the brain can also be referred to as procedural or muscle memory. Why do you think people seldom forget how to ride a bike, how to type, how to play the piano, or how to drive a car with a standard transmission even though they have driven an automatic for years? I was teaching one of my classes when a participant related this story. Her mother has dementia and no longer recognizes her children or grandchildren. However, her mother is a pianist and still remembers how to play any selection she ever once played. That is the power of procedural memory, one of the strongest memory systems in the brain!

Here's another example. Did you see 2009 United States National Spelling Bee champion Kavya Shivashankar? She pretended to write each word on her hand before she spelled it for the judges. Not only did imaginary writing help to put the words in her procedural memory, but she was able to visualize the words as well. In the movie *Akela and the Bee*, Akela's ability to spell was enhanced by the procedural memory created as she jumped rope. Why do you think people love to sing the song "YMCA"? They get to do the movements that go along with the lyrics and it's tons of fun. When content is coupled with movement, not only does long-term memory improve, but learning also becomes engaging!

Seven action research projects were conducted, and all of them related that kinesthetic activities, such as movement, have the following advantages: (1) increase the brain's level of motivation; (2) create a positive state of learning; (3) raise test scores; (4) prepare the body and brain to learn; (5) increase the level of children's attention, engagement, and participation; and (6) assist children in more easily retaining and recalling information (Lengel & Kuczala, 2010). In fact, the person who is the most actively engaged in the learning is the one growing the most brain cells. Other researchers believe that real learning does not take place without movement since movement provides opportunity for the cerebellum to practice making the connections it will need for higher-level thinking (Hannaford, 2005).

Two brain-compatible strategies based on the body's ability to move are *role play* and the strategy of *movement* itself.

Role Play

When students act out or dramatize what they are learning, they are using role play. Role plays in the real world are used in many professional fields, such as counseling or psychiatry. A friend of mine related that on one job interview with a major company, he had to role play how he would deal with an

> Role play enhances enthusiasm, helps the brain recall information, and stores information in the body as well as the brain (E. Jensen, 2007).

irate customer. The person conducting the interview pretended that she was going to take her business away and he had to convince her to stay. He did it and, as a result, got the job! Have your children act out the steps in a math word problem or the definition of a vocabulary word. Have them make change or take measurements in math, which are additional role plays used to reinforce learning (Sprenger, 2007a).

Movement

I was teaching in Wiley, Texas, years ago when, during a discussion on procedural memory, a football coach experienced a revelation. He had always wondered why the very football players who were having difficulty retaining their content in class had no difficulty remembering every play on the field. He realized that in class, those students were sitting still watching the teacher do all the work, while at football practice, they were actively engaged in the exercises and the plays being taught. In fact, one research study found that when students participated in aerobic exercise vigorous enough to raise the heart rate at least three times per week, their performance on classroom assignments actually improved (Rodriguez, 2007).

The brain and body are made for movement. We are designed to stand, sit, stoop, squat, dance, hop, skip, and jump. Yet in many classrooms, students are made to sit for long periods of time devoid of activity, and then teachers wonder why some of those students are up and out of their seats at inappropriate times. Movement not only helps with procedural memory, but it assists with reading, gets more glucose and blood to the brain, changes the mood of the brain, and provides tons of fun during learning (Sprenger, 2007b). The book *Brain Gym* by Paul and Gail Dennison (1992) contains numerous physical activities that enable the child to cross the midline of the body. Research has shown that this technique increases memory since when the midline of the body is crossed, the left and right hemispheres work together better than ever. Get your children up and moving when doing homework and watch their memory for content improve. Learning with boys especially is most productive when a great deal of *doing* and

> The only known cognitive activity that uses 100% of the brain is probably physical performance (Jensen, 2008).

competition are involved rather than just listening and observing (Nagel, 2006). Not only will test scores and grades improve for all students, but homework time can also be more fun than drudgery.

HOW CAN I MAKE IT HAPPEN?

○ Use the book *A, My Name Is Alice* by Jane Bayer (1984) to teach beginning consonant sounds in words. The illustrations in the book are also wonderful. Read the story aloud to your children and notice the language pattern. For example, the second verse is:

> B, My name is Barbara.
>
> And my husband's name is Bob.
>
> We come from Brazil.
>
> And we sell balloons.
>
> Barbara is a BEAR.
>
> Bob is a BABOON.

Once they understand the pattern, have your children make up rhymes using the beginning sounds of their own names. I even created the following rhyme from my name:

> M, My name in Marcia.
>
> And my husband's name in Marvin.
>
> We come from Maryland.
>
> And we sell macaroni.
>
> Marcia is a mackerel.
>
> Marvin is a Maltese.

The book enlarges vocabulary by exposing children to animals that they may not already know. It is also a lot of fun to go outside and have your children jump rope to the rhyming pattern in the book (Tate, 2010).

○ Put some movement into homework practice. For example, to help your children distinguish between common and proper nouns, have them stand if you read a proper noun (such as *Wal-Mart*, *Mrs. Williams*, or *Florida*) and sit down if you read a common noun (such as *door*, *chair*, or *pencil*).

○ Have students jump rope or clap while skip-counting during math homework. Have them count by 2s, 3s, 5s, 10s, or 20s as they jump or clap.

○ When helping your children review vocabulary words in any content area, have them get up and act out, or role play, the word. Obviously, verbs would work better with role play, but many other parts of speech can be acted out as well. For example, to show you that they know the definition of the word *petrified*, your child could look extremely scared.

○ Have your children role play, or act out, each step in an appropriate multistep mathematics word problem.

○ Take abstract concepts taught in school and make them more concrete by having your children act them out in the real world. For example, when my daughter Jennifer was having a difficult time remembering the quantities of measurement for cups, pints, quarts, and gallons, I took her into the kitchen and had her actually pour water from one size container to another. All of a sudden, the concept made sense and she made an *A* on the test several days later.

○ Teach students to use their bodies to *body-spell* vocabulary words. They will make a good grade on every spelling test and their spelling should improve when writing as well. To body-spell, either write the word on a piece of paper as a visual or have them visualize the word, or see it in their mind. Have them move their bodies according to the placement of the letters in the word. For example, let's body-spell the word *play*. The lowercase *p* in *play* falls below the line, so to body-spell it, your child should bend toward the floor from the waist with the arms extended as if to touch the toes. The *l* in *play* extends above the line, so to body-spell it, have your child put both arms up and reach for the sky. The *a* in *play* falls on the line, so your child should extend both arms out to the sides. Finally, the *y* in *play* falls below the line (just like the *p*), so have your child position the arms once again to touch the toes. Now put it all together and have him or her body-spell the entire word *play*. Have them say each letter of the word as they spell it. Once your children know the technique, they can spell any word, including *photosynthesis*. Have them spell the word faster and faster. What they don't realize is that the spellings are being placed in one of their strongest memory systems, and their spelling grades should improve (Tate, 2010).

○ When reviewing vocabulary words with your children, play the game of Charades. Write the words to be reviewed on separate index cards. Have each child select a card at random and then act out, or role play, the definition. Your child cannot speak but can only use gestures to get you to say the word. Once the word is guessed, it becomes your turn to act out the next word while your child guesses. Continue until all the words have been reviewed several times. Repetition is good for the brain!

○ Have your children dramatize part of a story that you have previously read to them or that they have read themselves. If the plot calls for more than one character, have family members help in the role play.

○ It is crucial that stimuli be changed for students because the amount of time a student can focus is equal to the age of the student in minutes (DeFina, 2003). Therefore, when your children are doing homework that takes a great deal of time, allow them to take stretch breaks. You can even put on slow- or fast-paced music and lead them in a series of stretches or exercises periodically between study sessions.

ACTION PLAN

> What will I commit to do to strengthen my
> child(ren)'s kinesthetic mode of learning?

What am I already doing that I should continue to do?

1. _____
_____
_____.

2. _____
_____
_____.

3. _____
_____
_____.

4. _____
_____
_____.

What new habits will I commit to developing?

1. _____
_____
_____.

2. _____
_____
_____.

3. _____
_____
_____.

4. _____
_____
_____.

Strengthen Your Child's Tactile Mode of Learning

Tell me, I forget!

Show me, I remember!

Involve me, I understand!

—Old Chinese Proverb

WHAT DOES THAT MEAN?

Another way to involve the body is through what researcher Howard Gardner (1983) refers to as visual–spatial intelligence. If you are in my age range, you may remember the game of the Rubik's Cube where the objective was to manipulate the individual cubes until each side of the cube was one color. I could never do it! However, many people could.

Many brains in the real world that possess visual–spatial intelligence turn out to be artists, architects, surgeons, and scientists.

The use of the hands and activity in the brain is such a complicated connection that no one theory explains it (E. Jensen, 2001).

Many children are hands-on learners and retain content better if they have an opportunity to use the three additional brain-compatible strategies of writing, drawing, and manipulatives.

Writing

Have you ever written down a list of groceries that you wanted to get at the store and then left the list at home? Isn't it amazing that you probably remembered most of the things on the list when you got to the store simply because you wrote them down ahead of time? There may be a biological reason for this phenomenon. Acetylcholine, a neurotransmitter that aids the brain in forming long-term memories, is released when neurons connect through speech and through writing (Hannaford, 2005). Recently, my daughter and I gave a baby shower for a relative on a Saturday. On the Friday night prior to the shower, I wrote down everything I still had to do to get ready. I never looked at the list once but accomplished everything that was on it.

Writing not only helps the brain remember but it also enables children to become more proficient with language. If you really think about it, there are really good readers who are not necessarily good writers, but have you ever heard of an excellent writer who was not also a good reader? Children need consistent and constant chances to write, to write some more, and to write some more if they are to become skillful with written language (Fogarty, 2009).

Another use of the written word is in a personal journal. When children have an opportunity to write down an account of an important event or occurrence in their lives, they are better able to process and understand their feelings related to that occurrence. Research supports that writing in a journal helps the brain make meaning out of new information (E. Jensen, 2007) and, actually, the very best way to remember the details of an experience is to write down an account of it immediately after it happens (Markowitz & Jensen, 2007).

Drawing

I cannot tell you the number of times I have observed in classrooms and watched students, especially boys, engaged in off-task behavior, drawing superheroes, cars, and tennis shoes while teachers conducted class in the front of the room. More than 70 years ago, an educator by the name of

> When some children have trouble visualizing, they may need to draw pictures (Eide & Eide, 2006).

John Dewey wrote about the positive relationship between thinking in art and thinking across the curriculum (Dewey, 1934). Today, the brain research concurs with his findings. When people are involved in art activities, different areas of the brain, such as the thalamus and the amygdala, are activated (E. Jensen, 2001). Anything we draw we have a better chance of remembering. Many adults doodle as they sit in meetings or talk on the phone. Many children do the same thing. You can use this talent to your children's advantage.

Manipulatives

When my daughter Jennifer was in 10th grade, she took chemistry. As I followed her progress, I noticed that she achieved 100% on every laboratory assignment in class. However, when I attended parent–teacher conference night, I was told that she was not doing as well on paper–pencil tests. Jen's lab grade only constituted 10% of her overall semester average. Now here is a question for you. What do real chemists do? How many children are convinced that they cannot be chemists since they can do the lab work that real chemists do but may not do as well on objective tests? It appears that the brain never outgrows its need for the hands. Manipulatives can assist even high school students in accelerating their ability in mathematics (Curtain-Phillips, 2008) as well as science.

While I am trying to change the way teachers view their instructional practice, parents can use these tactile strategies to their advantage while working with their children at home. When your children do not appear to comprehend a concept that you are teaching them, have them count objects, build a model, or conduct an

> Children are developing a foundation for spatial sense when they are working with concrete shapes (Wall & Posamentier, 2006).

experiment. This practice has the potential to help the learning make sense!

HOW CAN I MAKE IT HAPPEN?

○   The brain tends to remember what it writes down. Preschool children will want to draw or sketch, but school-age children can engage in quick writes. Take time when helping with homework to allow your children to write down words or concepts they need to remember.

○   Just as in any other skill, the more you practice it, the better you become. Give your children many real-life reasons to write. Allow them to write out your grocery list prior to a trip to the store. Have them write a to-do list for you or for themselves of things that need to be accomplished. Have them write a letter to Grandma or Grandpa or an aunt or uncle living in another city or state.

○   When children are writing, they often use words that they like over and over again and it makes their writing redundant and uninteresting. These are called *tired words* because they are so overused that they are tired. Examples of tired words in children's writing include the following: *said, good, pretty,* and *like.* Help them replace these tired words with others that make the writing more stimulating. Let us take the word *said.* Help them to brainstorm a list of all of the words that they can think of that mean about the same thing as the word *said.* These could include the following: *replied, stated, exclaimed, boasted, answered,* and *declared.* If you cannot think of other words, buy a thesaurus to help you. Keep these lists in a notebook for later reference. Then, when your children write, encourage them to use some of their new words in place of the tired ones.

○   Encourage your children to keep personal journals and to write daily about things that matter to them such as school, home, friends, challenges, and so forth. When I was young, the writing took place in diaries. Now they are called personal journals, and because they are personal, they are not read without the permission of the writer.

○   Have your children create a personal *pictionary* by illustrating vocabulary words they are trying to remember. Each page of the pictionary consists of a word, written in color, a drawing that shows the meaning of the word, and an original sentence that uses the word in context (Tate, 2010).

○   When helping your children with multiple meanings of words, have them draw pictures that represent the different meanings of the word. For example, you can remember four different definitions of the word *run* by drawing the following four pictures: a woman with a run in her stocking, a man running a race, a boy running his mouth, and a woman running for an elected office (Tate, 2005).

○ Buy a set of magnetic alphabet letters and while you are cooking dinner, allow your children to make words by placing the letters on the refrigerator. The tactile act of making the words enables them to remember. These letters will also stick to magnetic cookie sheets.

○ When reading aloud to your children, ask them to visualize, or see what is happening in the story in their minds. Then stop periodically and have them draw the scene they are visualizing. From their drawing, you can tell if they are comprehending the story.

○ Have your children draw each step in a multistep math word problem. Drawing is one of the primary strategies used by math teachers in Singapore, and those students have some of the highest math scores in the world.

○ Use foods found around the house as manipulatives (dry peas, beans, or macaroni) and have students move them around on the table while practicing adding, subtracting, multiplying, or dividing. For example, have them take 12 beans and divide them into groups of four. Help them to conclude that three groups of four make 12.

○ Have your children practice spelling or learning vocabulary words in the following tactile ways: writing the words in the air with the finger, writing them in shaving cream spread on the table, or making the words with clay.

○ If your children are working with multiplication facts, teach them that they have a human calculator right on their fingers, but it only works for the nine times tables. Have them hold their hands up in front of them (palm side facing away from the body) and spread their fingers. Starting with the little finger on the left hand, have your children assign a number to each finger. Have them turn down the finger that represents the number to be multiplied times nine. For example, if the student is multiplying nine times four, then the fourth finger on the left hand is turned down. All fingers to the left of the turned down finger is the first digit in the answer and all fingers to the right of the turned down finger is the second digit in the answer. Therefore, the answer is $9 \times 4 = 36$ (Tate, 2010, p. 58).

ACTION PLAN

What will I commit to do to strengthen my
child(ren)'s tactile mode of learning?

What am I already doing that I should continue to do?

1. _____
_____
_____.

2. _____
_____
_____.

3. _____
_____
_____.

4. _____
_____
_____.

What new habits will I commit to developing?

1. _____
_____
_____.

2. _____
_____
_____.

3. _____
_____
_____.

4. _____
_____
_____.

Make Memories With Music

Information stands a better chance of being encoded into long-term memory when that information is tied to music.

—E. Jensen, 2008

WHAT DOES THAT MEAN?

Music has many properties that can actually be miraculous for your brain and the brains of your children. It has the capability to perform three major functions. First, it can change the state of the brain. This function has been previously discussed in Chapter 3 for younger brains; however, this chapter will extend its use for brains of all ages. Second, it has properties that connect to other content areas such as mathematics and language. Last, it definitely helps you to remember. The paragraphs below elaborate on each function.

Music and State Changes

We talked in Chapter 3 about how classical, jazz, new age, or Celtic music can calm the brain for you as well as your children.

Allow me to relate two true stories that can serve as illustrations of how music can influence the brains of all ages.

Some years ago, Denise, a teacher in Livingston, Tennessee, told me of a mission trip she and a group of teenagers took to New Orleans to assist in the cleanup effort following Hurricane Katrina. Four vans took off from Tennessee with Denise driving one of them. She had informed her teenage passengers that they would be listening to hours of classical music on the way down. While the teenagers did not necessarily want to listen to the music, they had formed a relationship with Denise and wanted to ride with her. At each rest stop, the drivers of the other three vans were being harassed by the arguing, complaining, and constant harangue of their passengers. Denise commented that everyone in her van was asleep. The music affected the movement and mood of the teenagers and also helped their stressed brains relax (Sprenger, 2008). Calming music soothes even the teenage brain.

> Music has the remarkable ability to relax or energize, set the daily mood, stimulate children's brains, inspire, and make the learning fun (E. Jensen, 2009).

A second story was told to me by a teacher in Plymouth, Massachusetts. Rowena's mother was in the hospital dying of congestive heart failure and she had signed a living will that stated that she did not want to be kept alive on life supports. While the family was gathering and prior to the doctors disconnecting the life supports, Rowena recommended that they put earphones on her mother's ears and play some of her favorite inspirational music. Within 30 minutes, Rowena's mother's heart stabilized, and now, years later, she still lives. I have jokingly warned my husband to play my favorite music before he even considers doing anything similar to me. After more than 30 years or marriage, it will not be that easy to get rid of me!

Two stories both point to one fact, whether you are 8, 18, or 80: *music soothes the savage breast.*

The Math and Music Connection

My daughter Jessica had 10 years of piano lessons. She sight-reads music, played the trombone in the high school band, and sang in the chorus in high school as well. When she entered Vanderbilt University, she sang in the chorus and auditioned for and made the Chamber Chorus. To make the Chamber Chorus, one not only had to have a beautiful voice but also had to sight-read from a never-before-seen selection of music. She was able to do that. Coincidentally, Jessica also made a high score in the mathematics section of the SAT and speaks fluent German. She was a German major at Vanderbilt.

The connection between her ability to sight-read music and play instruments, her high score in math, and her second language ability just may not be a coincidence. All three of those processes appear to be controlled by the spatial part of the brain.

Though the ability to play a musical instrument may begin around age 3, babies actually respond to music in utero (Sprenger, 2008). This is one reason why Japanese parents in my classes tell me that they have their children taking instrumental music lessons like Suzuki violin. In fact,

> Of all of the content areas, mathematics appears to be the one most closely aligned to music. Music uses patterns for notes and chords, counting for beats, and rests, ratios, proportions, fractions, and geometry for placement of the fingers on the guitar (Sousa, 2006).

every country with the world's highest science and mathematics scores also has strong music and art programs (E. Jensen, 2008). Even the mathematics scores of low-socioeconomic students more than doubled for those who took music lessons compared to those who did not (Catterall, Chapleau, & Iwanga, 1999).

Music and Memory

Music can also help you and your children remember. Finish this phrase, *Conjunction junction,* _____. If you said *What's your function?* you fall into the *Schoolhouse Rock* generation. If you couldn't finish the phrase, it simply means you are too young to recall when music and cartoon characters taught concepts on Saturday mornings in a show called *Schoolhouse Rock*. Guess what? It worked! I still remember learning the steps in how a bill became a law, the parts of speech, or the Preamble to the Constitution, all put to music.

The military knows about the power of music for memory. The true story is told about a serviceman named Douglas Hegdahl. Douglas was captured during the Vietnam War

> The brain seems to be specialized for music since brain cells process the contour of the melody and the auditory cortex responds to pitch and tones (Weinberger, 2004).

and taken to a prisoner-of-war camp known as the Hanoi Hilton. Since Douglas was eventually going to be released, he was asked to remember the names of as many prisoners of war at the Hanoi Hilton as possible so that their families could be notified. They had him recall the names by singing them to the tune of *Old MacDonald Had a Farm.* When he was released, Douglas sang the names of over 200 POWs. This task was made much easier thanks to the power of music for memory in the brain.

Teachers and parents will tell me that their children cannot remember content when those same children are proceeding down the hall at school or dancing at home while singing the lyrics to every song, rhyme, or rap that comes on the radio. There is nothing wrong with these children's brains, and music helps them remember. Children can easily learn words to new songs since the rhythms, contrasts, and patterns of music help the brain encode new information (E. Jensen, 2005). Use this strategy to your advantage by using the activities that follow in this chapter.

HOW CAN I MAKE IT HAPPEN?

o When your children are getting restless or aggravated or if you would just like to experience some peace and quiet, put on some calming music. Types of calming music include smooth jazz, classical, Celtic, new age, Native American, and nature sounds. Try this type of music on a long road trip in the car or at naptime for your children.

o High-energy music can be very motivating! Give your children a task to do, particularly one that they do not find too appealing, and tell them that the task needs to be completed before a selected, fast-paced song ends. As I travel, I see signs in bathrooms that use this approach. They state that to know if you are washing your hands long enough, you should be able to simultaneously sing the entire song "Happy Birthday to You" once while washing.

o Do you ever wonder why some children, particularly teenagers, appear to stay angry, annoyed, or aggravated? Part of the answer may lie in the type of music to which they consistently listen. Music containing lyrics that reflect profanity, violence, or other types of negativity can negatively impact one's disposition. If your children are well grounded, listening to some of these lyrics does not appear to be detrimental. However, when other issues already exist in the brain, these can be exacerbated by the oppositional lyrics in certain types of music.

○ Since there appears to be some relationship between the brain's ability to do higher-level math and its ability to play a musical instrument, provide opportunities for your children to learn to play a musical instrument. Some children may become very interested and develop their talents in this area while others may not. Of my three children, only one enjoyed 10 years of piano lessons. The others gravitated to other interests. Remember, different children have different gifts, but they may never know what those gifts are if they do not try a variety of experiences!

○ Create a song or rap to help your children remember a concept they need to recall. Sing it to your children and have them sing it back to you numerous times. The music will help the brain remember.

○ If your children are old enough, have them create their own song or rap to help them remember the definition of a vocabulary word or a major concept to be recalled. When brains are creating information in a new form, such as a song, they are using synthesis, one of the highest-level thinking skills. As they sing the song, they will remember the information.

○ Use music to introduce or review specific content by getting rock, rap, or country CDs from the company Rocknlearn. Each CD is packaged with a book and can be found at a local teacher store or by logging on to www.rocknlearn.com. Topics on these CDs include addition, subtraction, multiplication and division facts, historical events, and phonics skills.

○ If you want your children to know a great deal of science, log on to Warren Phillips's website at www.wphillips.com. Warren Phillips, a retired exemplary middle school science teacher from Plymouth, Massachusetts, has written songs on three CDs called *SingAlongScience*. These CDs are designed to help students learn a myriad of different science concepts. The songs are common tunes, but the lyrics, written by Warren, are creatively clever. Watch how much science your children can learn once they start singing these songs!

○ Dr. Jean Feldman is another good resource for learning concepts through music, particularly with younger children. You can find her songs by googling "Dr. Jean Feldman songs" or "Dr. Jean Feldman music" on the Internet.

   ○ Since the brain likes rhythm, have your children clap, slap, or stomp out what they are learning. For example, they could clap the syllables in a vocabulary or spelling word. The word *dog* deserves one clap while the word *refrigerator* would get five.

   ○ The brain remembers rhyme, which is why Mother Goose nursery rhymes have sustained their popularity for generations. Older children can also create rhymes that will help them remember content. Have your children take what they are trying to recall and turn it into a catchy rhyme. Then add a little rhythm for good measure.

ACTION PLAN

> What will I commit to do to show my child(ren)
> the benefits of music for learning?

What am I already doing that I should continue to do?

1. _____
_____
_____.

2. _____
_____
_____.

3. _____
_____
_____.

4. _____
_____
_____.

What new habits will I commit to developing?

1. _____
_____
_____.

2. _____
_____
_____.

3. _____
_____
_____.

4. _____
_____
_____.

Connect Content
With Your
Child's Life

The chances that new information will be remembered are increased when that information is connected to relevant issues.

—Sprenger, 2005

WHAT DOES THAT MEAN?

What came first—schools or brains? Of course, human beings had brains long before there were formal schools. Since the purpose of the brain is survival in the real world and not to make straight As or score high on the SAT in school, when students cannot see the relationship between what is being taught in school and their personal lives, they will ask their teachers, *Why do we have to learn this?* For this reason, when you are working with your children at home, if you can find a way to relate what you are trying to get across to them to their personal lives, the learning appears to *stick better* and they tend to remember the concept.

If content is irrelevant, one neuron in the brain will not likely connect with another neuron to promote understanding (E. Jensen, 2008).

There is a biological reason for why content needs to be relevant. The brain's nerve cells seldom move; therefore, to make a connection, the cells extend their axons to connect with the dendrites of another cell. When the connections are not made, it is difficult to establish relevance, yet these connections are what form our thinking, consciousness, and personality (E. Jensen, 2008).

Here are two new examples of ways to connect content with the real world. I was teaching a lesson on dominant and recessive genes to a group of sixth graders, and I told the class the following true story. My father was born with the trait for sickle cell anemia. He passed it to my older sister, Ann, who also has the trait. She has passed it genetically to her daughter, Erica. I do not have the trait. My daughter Jennifer does not have the trait, but my granddaughter, Jennifer's daughter Aidan, does. Therefore, my niece and my granddaughter will have to watch who they marry. If they marry someone who also has the trait, they will have a chance of having a child with sickle cell anemia. Students in my class then saw the relevance for my subsequent lesson on the effects of dominant and recessive genes.

To teach the concept of ways in which the layers of the earth settle, I compared the layers to the way clothes are thrown in a laundry basket. I asked students the following question: *When you are throwing clothes in a laundry basket over a period of time, where are the clothes that have been thrown in most recently?* They responded, *On the top!* Then I reminded them that this is the exact same way that sediment settles on the earth. The concept then became easier for students to understand.

Two brain-compatible strategies on our list of 20 take full advantage of the brain's need to connect information. They are the strategies of metaphor, analogy, and simile and the strategy of mnemonic devices. Both are discussed in the paragraphs that follow.

Metaphor, Analogy, Simile

One of the best instructional strategies to use when helping your children understand a concept being taught in school is the concept of *metaphor, analogy, and simile*. When you can take a concept and connect it to another concept your child can easily recognize, understanding and retention occur. When you use a *metaphor,* you compare two things without the use of *like* or *as.* An example of a metaphor would be as follows: *The*

> The concept of metaphor uses something familiar to explain something unfamiliar and something tangible to explain something conceptual (Jones, 2008).

brain is a chain because it has many links. When children make connections with metaphors, their thinking is stretched and their understanding is increased (Gregory & Chapman, 2002). An *analogy* tells how two things are alike. For example: *A referee is to football as an umpire is to baseball.* Analogies can be invaluable since they give insight into students' inaccuracies and misconceptions regarding their knowledge of content (Keeley, 2008). In fact, very complex ideas can be conceptualized when explanations are provided with analogies (Posamentier & Jaye, 2006). A *simile* compares two or more things using the words *like* or *as.* For example: *He was as quiet as a mouse.*

This strategy is used a great deal in the real world to help people see connections. For example, finish this phrase, *"Like sands through the hour glass _____.* The answer is *so are the days of our lives.* What about this commercial: *Like a good neighbor, State Farm is there.* I even use a simile when I teach the concept of *main idea.* I tell students that a main idea is like a text message. When you text someone, you have to give them the most important information. You cannot supply them with too many details. That becomes too expensive. Like a text message, the main idea of a story should tell you the most important concepts or events in the story. By the way, something funny happened when I was teaching in Los Angeles. I told a group of sixth graders the same story comparing a text message and the main idea, relating that additional details can become too expensive. One student replied, *It's not expensive! We have the family plan!* So much for my comparison!

Mnemonic Devices

Another strategy that helps the brain connect ideas together is the use of mnemonic devices. The word *mnemonic* comes from the Greek word *mnema,* which means *memory,* and uses the principle of association. Recall and retention are increased when students are provided with a mnemonic aid (Ronis, 2006).

Two types of mnemonic devices are acronyms and acrostics. An acronym is a word in which each letter in the word stands for the concept to be remembered. For example, to remember the Great Lakes, remember the word *HOMES* (**H**uron, **O**ntario, **M**ichigan, **E**rie, and **S**uperior). An acrostic is a sentence in which the first letter in each word of the sentence actually represents the first letter in the concept to be memorized. For

> When people depend on mnemonic devices, learning is increased two- to three-fold (Markowitz & Jensen, 2007).

example, to recall the lines on the treble clef of a musical staff, which are *EGBDF,* remember **E**very **G**ood **B**oy **D**oes **F**ine.

Acrostics trigger students to remember content, but they may need help connecting the acrostic to the material to be remembered (Allen, 2008). That's where you, the parent, come in.

HOW CAN I MAKE IT HAPPEN?

○ When helping your children with homework, take a concept they are trying to remember and connect it to their lives. Tell them when and where they will see this concept in the real world. That teaching technique alone will make it easier for your children to recall the concept. For example, when teaching the concept of fractions, compare the concept to the pieces in a pizza. Either show your children a real pizza or draw a pizza and talk about the number of slices that would comprise a whole, half, fourth, and eighth. Another example could occur when teaching your children to count money. Use actual change and have them count out the amounts of money it would take to buy certain items in your kitchen cabinet.

○ When helping your children write a paragraph, tell them that a paragraph should have a main idea and details. Compare this concept to a table with four legs. Tell your children that the top of the table is the main idea. But, like the main idea, the top of the table does not stand up by itself. It is supported by legs. Tell them that in their paragraph, the main idea is the top of the table and the legs are the supporting details. Then have them draw a table with four legs and, before they write the actual paragraph, have them write their main idea on the top of the table and one detail on each of four legs.

○ Use similes to connect things together. A simile compares two or more concepts with the use of the words *like* or *as*. For example, *She was as angry as a wet hornet. He runs as fast as a rabbit.* Help your child find examples of similes in the real world and use similes when teaching to make an unfamiliar concept familiar.

○ Use analogies to help children visualize similarities. An analogy compares two or more things using the following formula: *a : b :: c : d*, which reads, *a* is to *b* as *c* is to *d*. For example, *Shakespeare: Romeo and Juliet : : Charles Dickens : A Tale of Two Cities.* Play a game of seeing how many real-life analogies your children can create on their own or look for analogies that present themselves when helping your children with homework.

○ Use metaphors to increase understanding. A metaphor compares two or more things without the use of the words *like* or *as.* For example, the poet Carl Sandburg used a metaphor when he wrote *The fog comes in on little cat feet* to compare the quiet arrival of the fog to the quiet arrival of a cat coming into a room. Help older children make connections through the use of metaphors since these are often more difficult to understand than similes or analogies.

○ Use acronyms to help children remember content. Mnemonic devices connect ideas together into words or sentences. When ideas are connected in a word or initials it is called an acronym. An example would be to remember the word **ROY G. BIV** for the colors of the spectrum: **r**ed, **o**range, **y**ellow, **g**reen, **b**lue, **i**ndigo, and **v**iolet. Help your children remember important content by providing them with acronyms.

○ A fun activity to do with your children is to turn them into detectives and have them find all of the acronyms they can in the real world. When you really look for them, acronyms and acrostics are everywhere. Some examples would include the following: AIDS, SIDS, SCUBA, IRS, NFL, NASA, or CIA.

○ Use acrostics to help children remember concepts. An example would be **My very educated mother just served us nine pizzas,** which used to be the planets in order from the sun **M**ercury, **V**enus, **E**arth, **M**ars, **J**upiter, **S**aturn, **U**ranus, **N**eptune, and **P**luto. Since we have lost Pluto, I have changed this acrostic to **My very educated mother just served us nachos.** We stop with Neptune. If your children are young, create acrostics that will help them remember concepts for later recall. Make certain that they understand the concept so that the acrostic makes sense.

o If your children are older, have them create their own mnemonic devices to help them remember. Mnemonic devices are of benefit to the brain but are more meaningful if students create their own rather than memorizing the devices provided (Feinstein, 2009). For example, I was teaching the order of operations in math, which is *Please excuse my dear Aunt Sally* (**p**arenthesis, **e**xponents, **m**ultiple, **d**ivide, **a**dd, **s**ubtract). One middle school student wrote his own acrostic to help him remember this concept. His original acrostic was *Please end my day at school!*

ACTION PLAN

> What will I commit to do to connect content
> to my child(ren)'s lives?

What am I already doing that I should continue to do?

1. _____
   _____
   _____.

2. _____
   _____
   _____.

3. _____
   _____
   _____.

4. _____
   _____
   _____.

What new habits will I commit to developing?

1. _____
   _____
   _____.

2. _____
   _____
   _____.

3. _____
   _____
   _____.

4. _____
   _____
   _____.

Partner With Your Child's Teachers

School leaders should provide a way for parents and teachers to create a unified vision of family engagement practices.

—Glasgow & Whitney, 2009

WHAT DOES THAT MEAN?

No doubt, you will remember the concept of the *emotional bank account* discussed in Chapter 1. This concept also applies to the relationship between you and your children's teachers. It is imperative that you work together with them to make decisions regarding what is best for your children. If you approach that relationship in a divisive manner, then you are making withdrawals from the bank account that you and your children's teachers share. If it continues, soon the account is overdrawn and ultimately experiences bankruptcy. This does not benefit either you or your children, since you will not want to go to the school and the teachers will not want to see you coming.

On the other hand, if you work together for what is best for your children, you will have established a strong bank account and great things can happen. In close to 40 years in education, I have noticed that when students begin school, most parents are

> A parent's involvement in the schooling of the child affects the child's achievement and, in turn, influences the career choices and educational goals of the child (Hill et. al., 2004).

consistently involved. They attend parent–teacher conferences, they are there for Parent Teacher Association (PTA) meetings, they volunteer as room mothers and fathers, and so forth. However, as students progress through the grades, parent participation wanes so that by the time students get to middle and high school, most parents don't perceive the need to be involved. In fact, many parents feel that they can be involved without ever going near the school since they are active parents in the home (Russell & Granville, 2005). That need for parental engagement still exists. In fact, it may even be more important as children get older!

At the other extreme, there are parents who think that, because they were once students themselves, they should be in a position to tell their children's teachers exactly what they should be doing and to make unrealistic demands. These parents also feel that, regardless of the situation, their child is always in the right. There are even those who come to school *loaded for bear*, who are antagonistic and demeaning to teachers. Remember that these actions put both the teachers' brains and your own into survival mode without the ability to make the best decisions for your child.

Having been a parent for more than 30 years and a teacher for almost 40, I have sat on both sides of a parent–teacher conference. One of the worst things you can experience as a parent is to hear troubling remarks about your child from his or her teacher, even if you know that they may be true. I feel qualified to share some recommendations on the most effective ways to work in your children's best interest.

> Even simple learning activities that children experience at home are effective ways that parents can use to help improve the academic success of their children at school (Parent Educational Tools, 2008).

HOW CAN I MAKE IT HAPPEN?

○ Be certain that the first interaction between you and your children's teachers is a positive one. During the first days or weeks of school, contact your children's teachers and make a deposit in their emotional bank accounts. Tell them how happy you are to be working with them and to do what is in the best interest of your children. As a teacher, I know that this first interaction means a great deal and sets a positive tone for the entire school year.

○ Schedule periodic conferences with your children's teachers. If your children are doing well, the conferences are important so that you know specifically what they are doing well. If your children are experiencing difficulties, you should know specifically what the challenges are so that you can work with the teachers in the best interest of improved academic achievement or behavior. When teachers know that a parent is truly interested in what is best for the child, there is increased motivation to work together.

○ Never let your children hear you criticize their teachers. If your children hear you say derogatory or condescending things about their teachers, it can diminish the amount of respect your children have for them. If there are things of which you do not approve, contact the teacher directly and, in a calm and respectful manner, let them know specifically of your concerns.

○ Volunteer to participate in some school-sponsored functions. Be a room parent, work at the fall carnival, or assist with a class holiday party. When your children actually see you participating in school-related activities, they will realize that school matters to you and should matter to them, and they will make more of an effort to do well.

○ More parents are engaged in their children's school activities when their children are in the lower elementary grades, such as kindergarten through Grade 3. However, as children get older, parents believe that they are no longer needed as advocates for their children and they stop attending school functions. It is not a high priority in their busy schedule. Make it a priority! It will pay big dividends. Remember to put first things first, Habit 1 of a highly effective person (Covey, 2004).

○ Volunteer to share your career choice or personal hobby or talent with the students in your children's school. When children understand how what they are learning in school relates to occupations in the real world, it makes the learning more relevant. Help students know what the possibilities are for future occupations in which they might be interested. For example, my daughter Jessica assistant to the chef at the Ritz Carlton Hotel in Atlanta, came to her sister Jennifer's class during career day and got third graders excited about pursuing a career in the culinary arts. She even cooked some simple dishes they could sample and talked about the importance of knowing measurement and math for this profession.

○ Many schools use agenda books. These work well for making parents aware of their children's homework assignments. Agenda books are calendars that enable students to write down their daily assignments. The books are then sent home so parents have an idea of what the homework assignments are. The parents sign the book to say that they have seen the assignments and send it back to school with the child. It is a great way for your children's teachers to keep in contact with you.

○ In this age of technological advances, there are computer programs that enable parents to go online and view their children's course syllabi, attendance, homework assignments, and grades. Find out if your children's school has such a program and if so, take advantage of it. In the school district I worked in for 30 years, DeKalb County School System in Decatur, Georgia, parents of students in this system can go to the school website at www.dekalb.k12.ga.us and, once online, they can click on *Parent Portal* and access this type of information for their children.

○ Some teachers have e-mail accounts set up through which they can keep in contact with their students' parents. Find out if this is one way that you can keep in touch with your children's teachers and, if so, use the service.

○ When parents have children who have learning or behavior challenges, working hand-in-hand with the school is essential. For example, school personnel can help ease the stress of parents who are raising a child with a learning disability by meeting personally with the parent as soon as the learning problems are detected and frequently communicating with the parent that all are working together to assist the student in meeting expectations (Sousa, 2007).

○ Do not automatically believe everything your children tell you about what is happening at school. Children who have chronic behavior disorders, such as conduct disorder or oppositional defiant disorder, may deliberately lie about a situation since they truly believe that nothing is ever their fault. Don't play into these misconceptions. I have also told teachers not to believe everything that a child says is happening in the home. If you have concerns, make an appointment and discuss those concerns with your children's teachers. It is absolutely essential that the lines of communication remain open.

ACTION PLAN

> What will I commit to do to partner with the
> teacher(s) of my child(ren)?

What am I already doing that I should continue to do?

1. _____
   _____
   _____.

2. _____
   _____
   _____.

3. _____
   _____
   _____.

4. _____
   _____
   _____.

What new habits will I commit to developing?

1. _____
   _____
   _____.

2. _____
   _____
   _____.

3. _____
   _____
   _____.

4. _____
   _____
   _____.

Afterword

Well, there you have it: the benefit of my close to 40 years as an educator and more than 30 years as a parent. Did you find all of the answers to your questions as a parent? Of course not! No one person has all the answers. Hopefully, you found some ideas to implement and the research behind why those ideas just may work for the brains of your children. By the way, did you also find the 10 things that keep adults living way beyond the age of 80 hidden in the chapters of this book? If you did not, here they are according to the American Association of Retired Persons (Mahoney, 2005):

Secrets for Long Life

1. Heredity—If your parents lived longer, you stand a better chance of living longer.

2. Purpose—People who have a specific reason to get up in the morning and stay active live longer.

3. Close Personal Relationships—People who are around other human beings (and pets, by the way) live longer.

4. Humor—People who laugh a lot (even fake laughter) strengthen their immunity and live longer.

5. Optimism—People who look at the positive side of life or *see the glass half-full rather than half-empty* live longer.

6. Exercise—People who keep their bodies engaged through physical activity (i.e., aerobics, walking, swimming, skiing, yoga, and so forth) live longer.

7. A Job You Are Passionate About—*If you love your job, you will never work a day in your life.* Your job will be play, not work, and you will live longer.

8. Music—People who learn to play a musical instrument or enjoy the powerful, positive effects of music live longer.

9. Games—You don't stop playing games because you grow old; you grow old because you stop playing games. Play and live longer.

10. Spirituality—People who believe in a higher power outside of themselves live longer.

Contractual Agreement

The following form can serve as a contract between you and your children. Review your action plans at the end of each chapter. Select three items to place on your contractual agreement that you think would make the most difference in your efforts to prepare your children for success either in life or in school or that you would like to work on to become a better parent. Work on those three things for 21 consecutive days or 28 times to make them habits in your brain. If your child is old enough, sit down and share your priorities and then work together so that they can identify their own priorities, which will help you accomplish yours. Once any of these things becomes a habit, select one or two others until you get to where you want to be.

For example, as a parent, your three priorities might be the following:

Priority 1: I will pledge to cook healthier meals for my family.

Priority 2: I will make more deposits than withdrawals in the *emotional bank accounts* of my children.

Priority 3: I will integrate the strategy of movement into the lessons when I am helping my children with homework.

Your child's priorities to complement yours might include:

Priority 1: I will make time in the morning to eat the healthy breakfast my parents prepare.

Priority 2: I will also make more deposits than withdrawals in the *emotional bank accounts* of my parents.

Priority 3: I will help to find ways to integrate movement into the lessons when I am doing my homework.

Remember one more thing. If you are going to do the best job of taking care of your children, take care of yourself first. I am on a plane three to five times most weeks, so I have heard the flight attendants' instructions on many occasions. They always say that if it becomes necessary, put on your oxygen mask before you put on the masks of your children. Why? You must take care of yourself first! Stephen Covey calls this Habit 7: *sharpen the saw,* since unless you keep your own blade sharp, you will not be effective at *cutting the wood* as a parent. Hopefully this book has helped you with the *sawing!*

CONTRACTUAL AGREEMENT

I, _____, commit to do the following for
      Parent's Name

the next **21 days** or **28 times (whichever comes first).**

Priority 1: _____

_____.

Priority 2: _____

_____.

Priority 3: _____

_____.

I, _____, commit to do the following for
      Child's Name

the next **21 days** or **28 times (whichever comes first).**

Priority 1: _____

_____.

Priority 2: _____

_____.

Priority 3: _____

_____.

_____   _____

Parent's Signature   **Child's Signature**

Bibliography

Adamson, L., Hartman, S. G., & Lyxell, B. (1999). Adolescent identity—a qualitative approach: Self-concept, existential questions and adult contacts. *Scandinavian Journal of Psychology, 40*(1), 21–31.

Algozzine, B., Campbell, P., & Wang, A. (2009). *63 tactics for teaching diverse learners: Grades K–6.* Thousand Oaks: CA: Corwin.

Allen, R. (2008). *Green light classrooms: Teaching techniques that accelerate learning.* Victoria, Australia: Hawker Brownlow.

Barkley, R. A. (2002). International consensus statement on ADHD: January 2002. *Clinical Child and Family Psychology Review, 5,* 89–111.

Bayer, J. (1984). *A, My name is Alice.* New York: Dial Books for Young Readers.

Bergen, D. (2006). *Early childhood.* In S. Feinstein (Ed.), *The Praeger handbook of learning and the brain* (pp. 187–192). Westport, CT: Praeger.

Caine, R. N., Caine, G., McClintic, C., & Klimek, K. (2005). *12 brain/mind learning principles in action: The fieldbook for making connections, teaching, and the human brain.* Victoria, Australia: Hawker Brownlow.

Caine, R. N., Caine, G., McClintic, C., & Klimek, K. J. (2009). *12 brain/mind learning principles in action: Developing executive functions of the human brain* (2nd ed.). Thousand Oaks, CA: Corwin.

Catterall, J., Chapleau, R., & Iwanga, J. (1999, Fall). *Involvement in the arts and human development: Extending an analysis of general associations and introducing the special cases of intense involvement in music and in theater arts* (Monograph Series No. 11). Washington, DC: Americas for the Arts.

Cline, F., & Fay, J. (2006). *Parenting with love and logic: Teaching children responsibility.* Colorado Springs, CO: Pinon Press.

Colbert, D. (2009). *Eat this and live! How to make simple food choices.* Lake Mary, FL: Siloam.

Costa, A. L. (2008). *The school as a home for the mind: Creating mindful curriculum, instruction, and dialogue.* (2nd Ed.) Victoria, Australia: Hawker Brownlow Education.

Covey, S. R. (1997). *The 7 habits of highly effective families.* New York: Free Press.

Covey, S. R. (2004). *The 7 habits of highly effective people: Powerful lessons in personal change.* New York: Free Press.

Curtain-Phillips, M. (2008). *How to make the most of math manipulatives—A fresh look at getting students' heads and hands around math concepts.* Retrieved August 31, 2009, from http://www.mathgoodies.com/articles/manipulatives.html.

Defina, P. (2003). *The neurobiology of memory: Understand, apply, and assess student memory.* Paper presented at the Learning and Brain Conference, Cambridge, MA.

Dennison, P., & Dennison, G. (1992) *Brain gym: Simple activities for whole brain learning*. Ventura, CA: Edu Kinesthetics.

Dewey, J. (1934). *Art as experience*. New York: Minion Ballet.

Dobson, J. (2001). *Bringing up boys: Practical advice and encouragement for those shaping the next generation of men*. Carol Stream, IL: Tyndale House.

Dowling, J. (2005). *Young children's personal, social, and emotional development*. (2nd ed.). London: Paul Chapman.

Eide, B., & Eide, F. (2006). *The mislabeled child*. New York: Hyperion.

Eliot, L. (2007, April). *What's going on in there? Nature, nurture, and early brain development*. Presentation at Learning and the Brain Conference, Cambridge, MA.

Emery, R. E., & Laumann-Billings, L. (1998). An overview of the nature, causes, and consequences of abusive family relationships: Toward differentiating maltreatment and violence. *American Psychologist, 53*, 121–135.

Erlauer, L. (2003). *The brain-compatible classroom: Using what we know about learning to improve teaching*. Alexandria, VA: Association for Supervision and Curriculum Development.

Feinstein, S. (2009). *Secrets of the teenage brain: Research-based strategies for reaching and teaching today's adolescents* (2nd ed.). Thousand Oaks, CA: Corwin.

Fogarty, R. (2009). *Brain-compatible classrooms* (3rd ed.). Victoria, Australia: Hawker Brownlow Education.

Fox, M. (2001). *Reading magic: Why reading aloud to our children will change their lives forever*. San Diego, CA: Harcourt.

Gardner, H. (1983). *Frames of mind: The theory of multiple intelligences*. New York: Basic Books.

Gibbs, N. (2009). Can these parents be saved? *Time, 174*(21), 52–57.

Glasser, W. (1990). *The quality school: Managing students without coercion*. New York: HarperCollins

Glasser, W. (1999). *Choice theory: A new psychology of personal freedom*. New York: HarperCollins.

Glasgow, N. A., & Whitney, P. J. (2009). *What successful schools do to involve families: 55 partnership strategies*. Thousand Oaks, CA: Corwin and National Association of Secondary School Principals.

Goleman, D. (1995). *Emotional intelligence*. New York: Bantam.

Gregory, G., & Chapman, C. (2002). *Differentiated instruction: One size doesn't fit all*. Thousand Oaks, CA: Corwin.

Gregory, G. H., & Parry, T. (2006). *Designing brain-compatible learning* (3rd ed.). Thousand Oaks, CA: Corwin.

Hannaford, C. (2005). *Smart moves* (2nd ed.). Salt Lake City, UT: Great Rivers Books.

Healey, J. (2004). *Your child's growing mind*. New York: Broadway.

Heschong Mahone Consulting Group. (2007). *Daylighting and productivity-CEC PIER*. Retrieved March 15, 2010, from www.h-m-g.com/projects/daylighting/projects-PIER.htm.

Hill, N. E., Castellino, D. R., Lansford, J. E., Nowlin, P., Dodge, K. A., Bates, J. E., et al. (2004). Parent academic involvement as related to school behavior, achievement, and aspirations: Demographic variations across adolescence. *Child Development. 75*(5), 1491–1509.

Hirsh-Pasek, K., & Golinkoff, R. (2003). *Einstein never used flash cards: How our children really learn and why they need to play more and memorize less.* Emmaus, PA: Rodale Press.

Jensen, E. (2001). *Arts with the brain in mind.* Alexandria, VA: Association for Supervision and Curriculum Development.

Jensen, E. (2005). *Top tunes for teaching: 977 song titles and practical tools for choosing the right music every time.* Thousand Oaks, CA. Corwin.

Jensen, E. (2007). *Brain-compatible strategies* (2nd ed.). Victoria, Australia: Hawker Brownlow Education.

Jensen, E. (2008). *Brain-based learning: The new paradigm of teaching.* Thousand Oaks, CA: Corwin.

Jensen, E. (2009). *Fierce teaching: Purpose, passion, and what matter most.* Thousand Oaks, CA: Corwin.

Jensen, E. (2010). *Different brains, different learners; How to reach the hard to reach* (2nd ed.). Thousand Oaks, CA: Corwin.

Jensen, E., & Dabney, M. (2000). *Learning smarter: The new science of teaching.* Thousand Oaks, CA: Corwin.

Jensen, R. (2008). *Catalyst teaching: High-impact teaching techniques for the science classroom.* Victoria, Australia: Hawker Brownlow Education.

Jones, C. (2008). *The magic of metaphor.* Retrieved April 6, 2010 from http://www.Uxmatters.com/mt/archives/2008/php

Keeley, P. (2008). *Science formative assessment: 75 practical strategies for linking assessment, instruction, and learning.* Thousand Oaks, CA: Corwin & National Science Teachers Association Press.

Kloske, G., & Blitt, B. (2005). *Once upon a time, the end: Asleep in 60 seconds.* New York: Atheneum Books for Young Readers.

Kluger, J. (January 17, 2005). The funny thing about laughter. *Time. 165*(3), A24–A29.

Kohn, A. (2005). *Unconditional parenting: Moving from rewards and punishments to love and reason.* New York: Atria Books.

Kottler, J. A. (2002). *Students who drive you crazy: Succeeding with resistant, unmotivated, and otherwise difficult young people.* Thousand Oaks, CA: Corwin.

Lakoff, G., & Johnson, M. (1980). *Metaphors we live by.* Chicago: University of Chicago Press.

Lengel, T., & Kuczala, M. (2010). *The kinesthetic classroom: Teaching and learning through movement.* Thousand Oaks, CA: Corwin.

Lewisohn, P. M., Rohde, P., & Seeley, J. R. (1998). Treatment of adolescent depression: Frequency of services and impact on functioning in young adulthood. *Depression and Anxiety, 7,* 47–52.

Markowitz, K., & Jensen, E. (2007). *The great memory book.* Heatherton, Victoria, Australia: Hawker Brownlow Education.

Mahoney, S. (2005, July/August). How to live longer. *American Association of Retired People, 48*(4B), 64–72.

Morrison, J. (1995). *DSM-IV made easy: The clinician's guide to diagnosis.* New York: Guilford.

Nagel, M. C. (2006). *Boys stir us.* Victoria, Australia. Hawker Brownlow Education.

Nelsen, J., Erwin, C., & Duffy, R. A. (2007). *Positive discipline: The first three years.* New York: Three Rivers Press.

Nemours Foundation. (2007). *Healthy habits for TV, video games, and the Internet.* Retrieved April 5, 2010, from http://www.kidshealth.org/parent/Positive/family/te-habits.html.

Nevills, P., & Wolfe, P. (2009). *Building the reading brain: PreK–3* (2nd ed.). Thousand Oaks, CA: Corwin.

Parent Educational Tools. (2008). *North Carolina Parent's Desk Reference.* Jacksonville, FL: Author.

Parker-Pope, T. (2010, May). Excerpt from *For better: The science of a good marriage. Reader's Digest,* 22.

Posamentier, A. S., & Jaye, D. (2006). *What successful math teachers do, Grades 6–12: 79 research-based strategies for the standards-based classroom.* Thousand Oaks, CA: Corwin.

Restak, R. (2001). *The secret life of the brain.* Washington, DC: Joseph Henry Press.

Rodriguez, A. (2007). *A day in the life of the brain.* New York: Chelsea House.

Ronis, D. L. (2006). *Brain-compatible mathematics* (2nd ed.). Thousand Oaks, CA: Corwin.

Runkel, H. E. (2007). *Screamfree parenting: The revolutionary approach to raising your kids by keeping your cool.* New York: Broadway Books.

Russell, K., & Granville, S. (2005). *Parents' views on improving parental involvement in children's education.* Edinburgh, Scotland: George Street Research for Scottish Executives.

Shaywitz, S. (2003). *Overcoming dyslexia.* New York: Alfred Knopf.

Sousa, D. A. (2006). *How the brain learns* (3rd ed.). Thousand Oaks, CA: Corwin.

Sousa, D. A. (2007). *How the special needs brain learns* (2nd ed.). Thousand Oaks, CA: Corwin.

Sousa, D. A. (2009). *How the brain influences behavior: Management strategies for every classroom.* Thousand Oaks, CA: Corwin.

Sprenger, M. (2007a). *Becoming a "wiz" at brain-based teaching: How to make every year your best year* (2nd ed.). Thousand Oaks, CA: Corwin.

Sprenger, M. (2007b). *Memory 101 for educators.* Thousand Oaks, CA: Corwin.

Sprenger, M. (2008). *The developing brain: Birth to age eight.* Thousand Oaks, CA: Corwin.

Stein, M. B., & Stein, D. J. (2008). Social anxiety disorder. *Lancet, 371,* 1115–1125.

Sternberg, R. J., & Grigorenko, E. L. (2000). *Teaching for successful intelligence: To increase student learning and achievement.* Arlington Heights, IL: Skylight.

Storm, B. (1999). The enhanced imagination: Storytelling? Power to entrance listeners. *Storytelling, 2*(2).

Sullivan, T. E., Schefft, B. K., Warm, J. S., & Dember, W. N. (1998, April). Effects of olfactory stimulation on the vigilance performance of individuals with brain injury. *Journal of Clinical and Experimental Neuropsychology, 20*(2), 227–236.

Sunderland, M. (2006). *The science of parenting.* New York: DK.

Tallal, P. (2007, March). *Better living through neuroscience.* Presentation at the Annual Conference of the Association for Supervision and Curriculum Development. Anaheim, CA.

Tate, M. L. (2005). *Reading and language arts worksheets don't grow dendrites: 20 literacy strategies that engage the brain.* Thousand Oaks, CA: Corwin.

Tate, M. L. (2007). *Shouting won't grow dendrites: 20 techniques for managing a brain-compatible classroom.* Thousand Oaks, CA: Corwin.

Tate, M. L. (2008). *Engage the brain games series: Grades K–6.* Thousand Oaks, CA: Corwin.

Tate, M. L. (2010). *Worksheets don't grow dendrites: 20 instructional strategies that engage the brain* (2nd ed.). Thousand Oaks, CA: Corwin.

Tileston, D. W. (2004). *Training manual for what every teacher should know.* Thousand Oaks, CA: Corwin.

Trelease, J. (2001). *The read-aloud handbook* (5th ed.). New York: Penguin Books.

Underwood, A. (October 3, 2005). The good heart. *Newsweek, 48*–55.

Wall, E. S., & Posamentier, A. S. (2006). *What successful math teachers do, Grades PreK–5: 47 research-based strategies for the standards-based classroom.* Thousand Oaks, CA: Corwin.

Weil, A. (2005, October 17). Aging naturally. *Time, 166*(16), 60–70.

Weinberger, N. M. (2004). Music and the brain. *Scientific American, 291*(5), 88–95.

Willis, J. (2006). *Research-based strategies to ignite student learning.* Alexandria, VA: Association for Supervision and Curriculum Development.

Wingert, P., & Brant, M. (2005, August 15). Reading your baby's mind. *Newsweek, 32*–39.

Wong, H. K., & Wong, R. T. (1998). *The first days of school: How to be an effective teacher.* Mountain View, CA: Harry K. Wong.

Index

CORWIN
A SAGE Company

The Corwin logo—a raven striding across an open book—represents the union of courage and learning. Corwin is committed to improving education for all learners by publishing books and other professional development resources for those serving the field of PreK–12 education. By providing practical, hands-on materials, Corwin continues to carry out the promise of its motto: **"Helping Educators Do Their Work Better."**